Streets
of Windsor
and Eton

Streets of Windsor and Eton

Third Edition
Edited by
Brigitte Mitchell

WINDSOR LOCAL HISTORY
PUBLICATIONS GROUP

The photograph on the front cover is of the Foot Guards
arriving at Windsor Castle for the state visit of the
President of South Africa and represents a familiar
sight on the streets of Windsor. It was taken on 12th June 2001
by Pamela Marson.
The photograph and drawing on the back cover are by Ken Byerley.
The map is John Roque's map of 1761.

Windsor Local History Publications Group was formed in 1976 from a small
group of WEA students and tutors with the aim of fostering research in the field
of local history and publishing the results.
Officers in 2003:
President: John Handcock, CVO, DL
Chair: Hester Davenport
Secretary: Brigitte Mitchell
Treasurer: Barbara Mitch

This book was first published in 1980 edited by Judith Hunter and reprinted.
The second edition (with updates) was published in 1995 edited by Pamela Marson.
This third edition (with further updates and additional photographs and maps) was
published in 2003 and edited by Brigitte Mitchell. Reprinted May 2004
The name of the group was changed to Windsor Local History Group at the AGM 2004.
256 Dedworth Road
Windsor SL4 4JR
and
56 Albert Street
Windsor SL4 5BU

Typeset by Pamela Marson
Cover design by Ken Byerley
Printed in England by Antony Rowe of Chippenham, Wiltshire, England
ISBN 0 9505 567 6 9

Acknowledgements

The Windsor Local History Publications Group is very grateful to everyone who has contributed to the updating of this publication. We should particularly like to thank Dr Brigitte Mitchell who has been a determined and indefatigable editor, discovering much new information and overseeing the rewriting and taking some of the modern photographs. Pamela Marson worked with her to find the illustrations, herself contributing some photographs including the cover picture. We are also much indebted to Pamela for giving her time and expertise to formatting the book for the printers. We are grateful likewise to Patrick Rooney for his work in liaising with the printer and for obtaining advertising.

We should like to express our thanks to Olivia Gooden for allowing us to search the files of the Royal Borough Museum Collection and to use pictures from it. We are grateful to the National Monuments Record for permission to reproduce several images from their collection. We would also like to thank Derek Hunt for providing the information on the VCs who are commemorated on the Broom Farm Estate and all those who helped to identify photographs.

The WLHPG would also like to acknowledge the help of the Royal Albert Institute Trust in underwriting the project.

Contents

Introduction
   original author Judith Hunter

Whither goes this road?   Brigitte Mitchell   9
The town by the castle gate   Judith Hunter   13
The ancient landscape   Joyce Sampson   23
Churches, chapels and schools   Judith Hunter   37
Kings, Queens and their relations   Beryl Hedges   47
   original author Carmel Finney

Tinker, tailor, soldier . . .   Hester Davenport   57
   original author Raymond South   Brigitte Mitchell   65

The lost streets of Windsor
   original author Gordon Cullingham   Brigitte Mitchell   77
And all the rest   Pamela Marson   85
The streets of Eton town   Selina Ballance   89
The village of Old Windsor
   original author Ann Brett   Margaret Gilson   95

Table of earliest dates of street mentions   104
Sources and key to illustrations   112
Index   11
Advertisements   124

Introduction

The naming of roads and streets in our towns and villages is a relatively recent necessity. Only after the establishment of the modern postal service in the middle of the nineteenth century, has it become essential for every street to have a name and every house a number. Of course the postal service goes back much further, but letters were usually paid for on delivery, and it was not cheap. In 1826 a letter from France cost 4s 8d per ounce. As more people became literate during the nineteenth century and wrote letters, the postal service expanded and in 1827 Windsor letter carrier William Tyler asked for more money. He was granted an increase in pay from 7s to 9s a week. The introduction of postage stamps made sending letters cheaper and easier. But not all letters carried the name of the road, as the postman was expected to know his customers; this 1841 letter to Windsor, stamped with the penny black, only carried the name of the recipient.

(GTc)

On other letters addresses were quite elaborate. In 1842 a letter was delivered to the Hope Inn on the Frogmore Road which carried the following instructions:

To the Landlord or Lady of the Public House situated
about 400 yard before the Market Place Windsor Berkshire
on the left hand side of the road from London by Datchet
and nearly opposite the foot path leading from
Datchet Bridge, through the Park to Windsor.

In 1911 the first aerial postal service in England went from Windsor to Hendon, and there is still an airmail post box on the junction of High Street, St Albans Street, Sheet Street and Park Street, just where Windsor's first post office used to stand. (See back cover)

(GTc)

Street names, however, go back a long way. Most towns had a High Street or Main Street and a Church Street, and many of the roads leading out of a town or village were called after the places they led to. The Datchet Lane obviously led to Datchet, and Sheet Street led to a field called the Sheet. Other streets were descriptive and told you about an activity or event that took place there, like Market Street or Mill Lane. The earliest map of Windsor to show some of the roads we are still familiar with is Norden's map of 1607 but the first map which gives the names of streets is Collier's plan of Windsor dated 1742. It shows a Gallows Lane in Old Windsor and a Pound Street in New Windsor; what stories do they tell? Other streets told you something about their immediate neighbourhood, like Brook Street or Barrack Lane. There have always been names which were simply nostalgic like Orchard Road and Willow Place, but there are also road names which make no sense at all or whose meanings have been lost or forgotten.

During the nineteenth century towns all over England expanded rapidly and Windsor was no exception. New roads were built for two reasons:

Firstly to connect neighbouring towns with better and faster roads. Many of these were constructed by the Turnpike Trust and often followed old tracks, of which the Dedworth Road and the Slough Road are two examples.

Secondly, new houses were built on land released by the Inclosure Acts or the sale of estates, like the Vansittart estate and the Keppel estate in Windsor. Some of the new roads that were created used commemorative names, and in the first place remembered the names of the estate holders, like Vansittart Road and Keppel Street.

High in popularity were names connected with the royal family, like Clarence Road, Victoria Street and Alexandra Road. Others remembered important events, like Alma Road.

In the twentieth century many of the Victorian streets in the Goswells between Peascod Street and the river were lost to slum clearance and new development, at the same time new estates have grown up to the west of the town, in Clewer and Dedworth. A large number of new street names were needed and for the first time Windsor honoured distinguished citizens of the past. Thus in the most modern part of the town we find streets named after mayors going back to the fifteenth century, after MPs, councillors, religious leaders, martyrs and other famous Windsorians. However, the new development in the centre of the town, Ward Royal, continued with the royal theme.

Over the years, some street names changed, either because of a change of use, or to stop confusion with another street or simply because the spelling changed. Fish Street became Church Street when fish was no longer sold there, St Andrew's Road became part of Duke Street, to distinguish it from St Andrew's Avenue and Crescent, and Peascod Street was at some time called Puscod or Pesecod Street.

The streets of our towns and villages can tell you much about their history, and we hope that *Streets of Windsor and Eton* will not only tell you why your street is so called, but also give you an insight into the long and fascinating history of your town.

(PM)

Whither goes this road?

Almost all the oldest surviving local place names are of Saxon origin. Certainly there were Celtic people living in the area, but they have left little evidence in the form of place names. Probably only the names of the River Thames and the village of Datchet have been passed down to us from those times. The meaning of the name Thames is very uncertain, but Datchet is derived from a Celtic word meaning wood. Within the area of modern Windsor, however, there were four Saxon villages or hamlets – Clewer, Dedworth, Losfield and Orton. All four are recorded as manors in the Domesday Book of 1086. Each name has a meaning. Clewer refers to its inhabitants, the dwellers by the cliff, and undoubtedly, the cliff referred to is the chalk bluff on which the castle stands. The Domesday entry for Clewer states quite clearly that part of that manor had been taken for the newly built castle. Moreover the Crown paid the Lord of the Manor twelve shillings a year rent for five hundred years!

The entry for Clewer in the Domesday Book which clearly shows the words castellum de Windesores *at the end of the third line and the beginning of the fourth line. (The line over the u signifies m)*

The word *worth* in the name Dedworth refers to an enclosure, probably the village green around which the village stood. The name Orton has long since been lost, though the village probably lay close to the castle hill, since the name means the village on the slope. The Domesday Book describes Losfield as a small manor, but its name suggests a much humbler origin, as a clearing in the forest for pigsties. In the seventeenth century it is recorded as the name of a meadow which lay near the parish boundaries, somewhere near Legoland. It is remembered in Losfield Road.

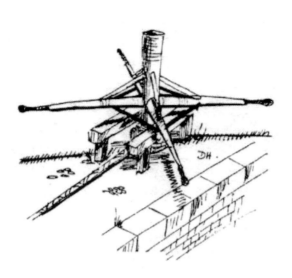

Winch (DH)

Windlass (DH)

The town of New Windsor was not founded until after the Norman conquest; before that the royal town of Windsor lay three miles downstream at Old Windsor. Its name means the river bank with the windlass; but why should the village be named after a device for lifting loads? There is no ready answer, certainly not for all the five or six places named Windsor in England. Could it be that the windlass was used to pull boats up the Thames over the shallows; or to unload boats for the palace, town or mill? There is no historical evidence for winches being used for hauling boats along the Thames in later centuries, and there is archaeological evidence for a large watermill at Old Windsor, but no evidence whatsoever of any windlass there. However, the name was adopted over nine centuries ago, and sadly our thoughts on the subject can only be speculative.

Several of the main routes through and away from Old and New Windsor and Eton have been named after places. Medieval references often mention ways leading to Datchet. The Datchet Road by the Windsor and Eton Riverside Station is probably the beginning of one of the oldest routes to Datchet across Underore Field to the town mill and thence to Datchet Ferry where the king's barge was sometimes moored. The road then known as Datchet Lane, is shown on Norden's Survey of 1607 and Collier's map of 1742 and several eighteenth century prints and paintings. In 1706 the ferry was replaced by a bridge, which had to be rebuilt three times until in 1851, the road to Datchet was realigned to cross the Thames via the new Victoria Bridge. Only a small section of the riverside route remains, a cul-de-sac called Romney Lock Road.

Datchet Lane looking towards Windsor (DF)

South of the Datchet Bridge, the road once known as the Datchet Road, led to Old Windsor, meeting the road which once passed through Frogmore to Windsor via Park Street. During the coaching era this was one of the routes for stagecoaches, wagons and post-chaises to Windsor from London. By this Frogmore route they avoided the hard haul up Thames Street hill. Like its northern counterpart this route to Datchet also disappeared when the Home Park was extended in 1851. It was replaced by the sweeping curve of the Datchet/Southlea Road which crosses the Thames by the Albert Bridge. Southlea was an area in Datchet parish; Southlea Farm is still there.

West of Windsor and Clewer Village is the Maidenhead Road. It too is an old road, which roughly divided the open arable fields from the water meadows by the Thames. In the eighteenth and nineteenth centuries, it was known as the Surly Hall Road after an inn of that name, much used by Eton College boys for strawberries and drinks. It would not have been known as the road to Maidenhead before about the thirteenth century for the town did not acquire the name until about this period. No doubt at times it was referred to as the road to Bray or the meadows. Surly Hall was commemorated by a small road off Dedworth Drive.

Many roads have derived their names from the towns and villages to which they led. There are scores of medieval references to Clewer Street – the road which led from Windsor to Clewer village. However, there is no longer a street of that name and what is left of the ancient road is now called by other names. By the nineteenth century it had become known as Clewer Lane and in 1869 by order of the Quarter Sessions it was straightened and realigned. The greater part of its remaining length was called Oxford Road. It was severed from its junction with Peascod Street by Ward Royal, part of the redevelopment scheme of 1966-70. The short section immediately west of the ancient junction was further shortened by the building of a new distribution road, connecting Goswell Road and Clarence Road. This road was given the name of a former road in the same area, Charles Street.

By the fourteenth century there were two villages in Clewer, the older by the parish church of St Andrew's, and the other, Clewer Green, on the higher land not far from the forest. There was no main street through the latter village, for like Dedworth its houses were built around a green. When this green was destroyed, as a result of the Inclosure Act of 1817, a new thirty foot wide road was made and called the Clewer Green Road. New houses were built and several mid-nineteenth century villas can still be seen. Sadly the name Clewer Green is now only the name of a school; the road was renamed Clewer Hill Road, possibly after one of the new houses, though it could be that the house was named after the road. The road does rise over a hill – by Windsor standards.

In 1819 Dedworth Green was also lost by enclosure and a new road laid out across its length in place of the more ancient track. It is called the Dedworth Road, though the greater part of it was not constructed until 1832 by the Windsor and Twyford Turnpike Trust.

Records of the early Middle Ages mention another hamlet and manor within Windsor's boundaries. This was Shaw. Its name means a small wood and it almost certainly lay within the wooded area of Windsor Forest. Most

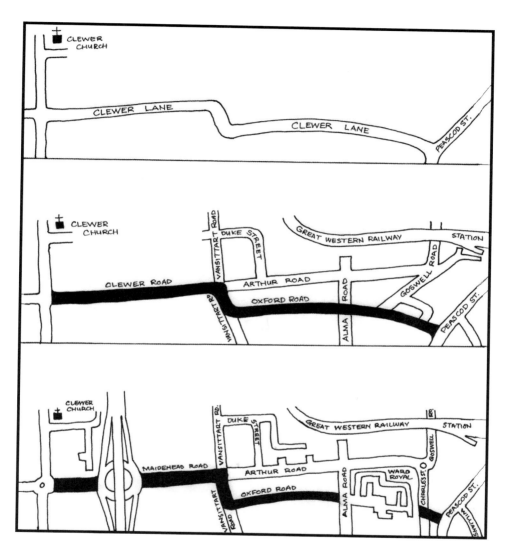

The Changing Road Pattern c1800, c1880 and c1980 (CG)

of Shaw was taken into the Great Park in the fourteenth century, but the road which led to that part of the park was still known as Shaw Lane until at least as late as the seventeenth century when it was shown on Norden's survey as Moat Park. It later became known as Sheet Street Road. There is, however, a Shaw Farm within the Crown Estates.

Curving south-west out of modern Windsor is the Winkfield Road. This would have been one of the main tracks through Windsor Forest, and it is shown on Norden's survey of the forest. Its route remained part of the waste and woodland of the forest until the Clewer Inclosure Act when its present route was determined. Winkfield itself is an ancient settlement which was recorded in a Saxon charter of 942; the name means Winca's clearing or village. However, although the track may always have led to Winkfield, deeds of the seventeenth, eighteenth and nineteenth centuries refer to the road as the road to Cranbourne Wood, the highway to Wokingham or the highway to the forest.

Eton too has its streets named from the places to which they lead – the Eton Wick and Slough Roads. Eton Wick began life as the place where the village livestock were kept, for *wick* is an Old English word meaning dairy farm. The name Eton means the village on an island, which was not an island in the river Thames, but an area of gravel which stood above the land which was flooded every winter. Slough on the other hand took its name from a quagmire, a muddy area, somewhere near the centre of the modern town.

As well as the several main roads which have been mentioned, there are a number of side streets incorporating place names, particularly those of Clewer and Dedworth. The oldest is Clewer Court Road, for although the houses are relatively new, the road itself dates back at least to the Middle Ages. Rocque's map of 1761 shows a road just south of the church and churchyard and later maps identify it with the beginning of Clewer Court Road. The first edition of the Ordnance Survey 50 inch map shows the parish stocks on its north side. However, the evidence for its age of six hundred years or more rests on one deed, part of the Brocas Collection in the Bodleian Library. It is concerned with the endowment of a small piece of land, later the site of the house called the Limes. The earliest reference to Clewer Court is in the Crown Revenue accounts of 1548 where it refers presumably to the manor house where the manor courts were held. By the nineteenth century the farmhouse to which the road led was known as Clewer Court Farm. It was demolished when the Windsor and Eton Relief Road was built. This opened in 1966.

Clewer Fields was laid out soon after 1817 and followed the line of an old footpath. It was a mean street which gained a reputation for poverty, squalor and immorality, and it was here that mission work was begun by the nuns of the House of Mercy in the 1860s. A very narrow street with foot access only, it marks the edge of the ordinary flood level.

Clewer Fields in 2003 is quite a fashionable area to live (BM)

In the late nineteenth century new housing districts built some distance from the old village were frequently called New Town. Clewer New Town began in this way; even in 1914 it was still a separate hamlet close to the cross roads of Dedworth Road and Parsonage and Hatch Lanes. The old cottages were demolished and replaced by modern council flats, but the name was retained. Clewer Avenue is the name of two twentieth century roads adjoining Clewer New Town, built for Windsor's first council houses about 1920. The houses were known as Addison Houses after the minister concerned with the relevant Housing Act of Parliament.

Clewer Park is a much newer road though it perpetuates an older name. Clewer Park was the home of Sir Daniel Gooch from 1859 to his

*The same view of Dedworth Road
in 1905 (above) and 2003 (below)
Immediately to the left of the picture is the Queen public house
and opposite now is Selwyn Close. (PM)*

death in 1889. He was an engineer and designer, who became chairman of the Great Western Railway Company. It was he who produced a steamship equipped to lay the first Atlantic cable. For this he was made a baronet, the first engineer to be so honoured. His house, Clewer Park, has been demolished, but a pair of estate cottages bearing his arms can still be seen in Mill Lane.

Clewer Park immediately before it was demolished (RBMC)

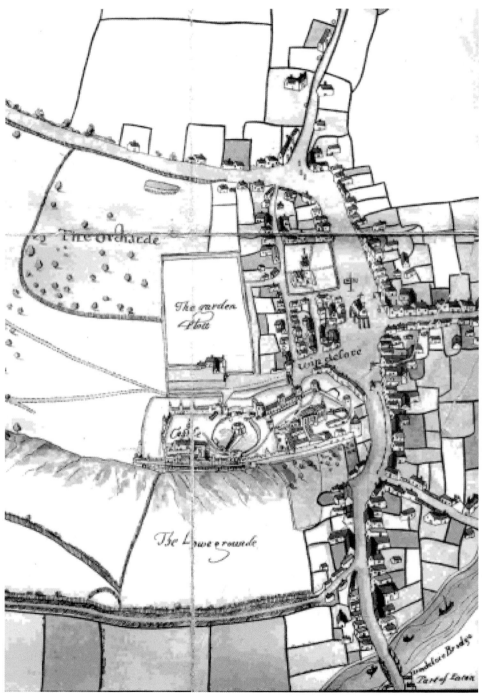

Part of the plan in Norden's Survey of Berkshire 1607 showing the Bridge between Eton and Windsor at the bottom and Park Street at the top.(RBMC)

The town by the castle gate

Henry I, the third of the Norman kings, initiated a programme of rebuilding at Windsor Castle from 1104 and in 1110 'held his court for the first time in the new Windsor'. The abandonment of the palace site of the Saxon and early Norman kings at Old Windsor some two miles downstream, in favour of the new castle, seems to have resulted in a migration of population.

The Domesday survey of 1086 had made no reference to a settlement at the castle gate but by 1121 there is a first mention of the growing little town of New Windsor. The first settlement was on the chalk outcrop immediately outside the castle gates but the town soon expanded to the south and down the steep northern slope to the river which was an important highway for men and goods. The development and growing importance of the town was recognised in the granting of Edward I's Charter of 1277.

The street pattern then established remained virtually unaltered until the rapid expansion of the town in the nineteenth century. The medieval town was small and even at the end of the sixteenth century the population was less than one thousand people. The next two centuries saw a gradual increase and by 1801 the population of Windsor and Clewer was 5,131, of whom 239 lived in the castle, 1,695 in Clewer and about 1,000 were soldiers. The constraints of the surrounding royal parkland and the susceptibility to flooding of the river plain encouraged redevelopment rather than expansion and the houses built in the seventeenth and eighteenth centuries to house the increased population were tall and narrow.

The Parish Church in about 1700 by Kip

The town was grouped around a triangular market place, the northern base of which faced the main gate of the castle, with the king's great garden, first mentioned in 1150, and vineyard on the east side, and on the west plots stretching to the Worth, one of the town's fields. The church of St John the Baptist, first mentioned in 1184 and rebuilt on the same site in 1822, occupied a central position in the market place. The regular street plan and the typical medieval triangular shape of the area suggest that it was deliberately laid out. In the thirteenth and fourteenth centuries tenements were interspersed with market stalls and booths. They were grouped according to trade: meat, fish, drapery, etc. which seems to have been an early feature of the market area.

The new streets were named after the markets which were held in them. Church Street was known for centuries as Fish Street and the earliest reference is in a lease of a shop 'next Fyssh Street' granted to Richard Hawle called Barbour in 1412. The street name and its associated market continued into the seventeenth century as shown by the following entry in the *First Hall Book* on 2nd March 1685, 'Fish Markett be removed from the Crosse and other places to the ancient place in Fish Street there to sell fish and not elsewhere'. The change to Church Street occurred in the latter part of the eighteenth century, the first mention being in a lease dated 1780.

Church Lane was also probably a medieval street but it is difficult to disentangle references to it from those for Church Street. A charity school, originally founded in 1705, was built in 1726 at the east end of Church Lane on the corner of the churchyard. The building ceased to be used as a school in January 1862 when the Free School united with the National School to form the Royal Free School which opened in new buildings on Bachelors Acre, and it was sold by the Trustees for use as a Masonic Hall.

Church Lane in 2003 with the Masonic Hall, the former Royal Free School (BM)

Until the nineteenth century Market Street was known as Butcher Row. An entry in the *First Hall Book* 5th October 1657 refers to the finishing of 'a well nere the Butcher Roe' and to the obligation on the 'parties or theire tenants shall continuallie maintain the same with rope and bucket at all times'. For a brief period during the early nineteenth century the street was called Queen Street as shown on a plan of 1811 of the property once known as the Rose and Crown and now the Edinburgh Woollen Mill. It is still named Castle Street on a map of 1848 although there is an early reference to the present name of Market Street in a report in the *Windsor and Eton Express* 27th June 1829 that the foundation stone of the enlargement of the Guildhall in Market Street was laid by J Eglestone Esq. This extension was built on ground leased for 'stallage of Markets & Fairs', the last lease of which terminated in Michaelmas 1831.

The ancient street of Castle Hill has only been known by that name since about 1850. Deeds in the possession of St George's Chapel and Eton College suggest that in the fourteenth and fifteenth centuries it may have been known as the King's Market Place and one deed dated 1436 is for a corner shop in a place called Merkatstede. In the seventeenth and eighteenth centuries the street, or at least the lower part of it up to the castle gate, was known as High Street as shown by the leases of the houses which were built in the castle ditch on the north side of the street. At the end of the eighteenth century the name was changed to Castle Street; the first mention of this new name was in a lease of a vault adjacent to the Horse and Groom dated 1796 and the change of name was also noted in the leases of the houses in the castle ditch.

St Albans Street was known in medieval times as Prest or Priest Street, presumably because the priest lived there. The earliest reference to Preste Street is in a deed dated 1379 and another deed dated 1392 refers to 'a messuage in Preste Street opposite the gaol'. There were houses on both sides of St Albans Street until the nineteenth century when those on the castle side were removed during George IV's alterations to the castle. Nell Gwyn and her descendants, the Dukes of St Albans, were perhaps the most illustrious residents of Priest Street. A lease of a small tenement and stable on the site of the Royal Mews was granted to 'Mrs El Gwyn, the Duke of St Albans, her son and succeeding Dukes' on 4th September 1665. In 1684 the Dean and Canons of St George's Chapel in two separate leases granted to 'Ellenor Gwinne of the parish of St Martin in the Fields Middlesex, one of the ladies of her Majesties the Queenes Privy Chamber, a messuage or tenement with backside garden and stable' and 'all their tenements, garden and orchard containing by estimation two acres more or less'. This second lease contains a reference to a 'great cartway to Rubbish Gate to northward' and may confirm TE Harwood's theory that Sheet Street originally continued to Edward III's Rubbish Gate. The Dukes of St Albans continued to live in Priest Street until the third Duke got into difficulties and in 1777 sold the house, later known as Burford Lodge, to Queen Charlotte. The street does not seem to have been given the name of St Albans until after the Dukes had left and the first mention of the change is in a lease of 1806.

Until the middle of the nineteenth century Park Street was an important thoroughfare and formed part of the road to London via Frogmore and Staines. It has been assumed that its medieval name of Mor or More Strate, first mentioned in 1315, was a reference to the mor meaning marsh at Frogmore but it may refer to a family surnamed de la More which had property here in the thirteenth century. The street was called Cuthorse Well Street in a deed dated 1583, and whilst the origin of this strange name is unknown, the Chamberlain's Accounts of 1635-7 record that 'post and rails were set about a well in More Street'. There is no need to speculate about its next name, Pound Street, which first appears in the Chamberlain's Accounts 1653 'rent of Mr Baker in Pound Street for the ground where the pound did stand'. Three houses, numbers 10, 11 and 12, were built on the site of the old pound (the local lock up) in Park Street in the nineteenth century and the 1795 lease of the ground, which refers to 'Moore Street, lately Pound Street now Park Street', is the first mention of the modern name of the street.

Between Sheet Street and Peascod Street lay a large tract of land called Le Worth. It seems to have been gradually reduced in size by the encroachments of gardens and slips of land on its edges, and Bachelors Acre is the last surviving remnant. The earliest reference by name to Bachelors Acre is in a lease of 1629 by the 'Provost of Our Blessed Lady of Eaton by Windsor to John Fishbourne of New Windsor of 3 acres of arable land in a field called the Worth ... adjoining at one side to pitts called Bachelors Acre' for a yearly rent of 2s plus ½ bushel of wheat and one bushel of malt or 'ready money for the same at the rate of best wheat and malt in Windsor Market'. The pits had been dug when marl was extracted at 'Pittsfield on Bachelors Acre, where the Butts are usually sett and made'. Every fit Windsor male used to practice archery here in the butts. A society of responsible townsmen, *The Bachelors of Windsor*, was founded in 1761 to safeguard the public amenities of the field.

*Drums and fifes of the 3rd Grenadier Guards in Victoria Street by
Bachelors Acre. In the background is the Infirmary. (BMc)
Below, Bachelors Acre in 2003. (BM)*

Contrasting views of Peascod Street
Above in the days before cars (RBMC) and below in
2003 after it had been pedestrianised (BM)

Peascod Street is probably one of the oldest streets in the town. The road follows a natural watershed and from earliest times it was a routeway between forest, castle and river crossing via the Datchet ferry to Colnbrook and thence to London. Considerable variations in the name of the street occur in the surviving thirteenth century leases, such as Puscroftstrate and Pescroftstrate. The first mention of Pesecod is in a lease of 1335 of a messuage 'stretching from Kingsway to a field called le Worthe'. In the fourteenth and fifteenth centuries Pesecod and Puscod were almost interchangeable. The name Peascod is derived from the croft where peas were grown. Peas and beans were an important part of the medieval diet. Norden in 1607 showed houses on both sides of Peascod Street and the Chamberlain's Accounts 1635 refer to 'paving a good part of the gutter in Peascod Street'. It is known that Richard Topham, Windsor's MP from 1698 to 1713, lived in Peascod Street early in the eighteenth century and it continued to be mainly residential throughout the eighteenth century. There were a number of side streets leading from Peascod Street such as Tulle Lane, Lammon Street and Sefstrate but they cannot now be identified. Sun Passage leading to Leworth Place and Goswell Hill are both shown on Collier's map of 1742. The 1851 Tithe map shows Goswell Hill, Acre Passage and Sun Passage and names the latter. Its continuation, now called Alexandra Road, follows an old field path.

The High Street, or Altus vicus as it is called in the earliest surviving lease of 1398, has long been the main street of the town. In the eighteenth century the south end was largely residential with many fine houses. Collier in 1742 named it Church Street but this name is not used in any of the deeds of the period. Its middle section was from ancient times the centre of Windsor's busy market. There is a reference to the market in Windsor in 1251 and thirteenth century deeds give details of booths and stalls in the market during the reign of Henry III (1216-72). In 1277 King Edward I granted New Windsor its first recorded Charter which, by making the town a free borough and its 'good men' free burgesses, contributed greatly to the growth and prosperity of the town. It seems appropriate that shortly after the celebrations to mark the Charter's sept-centenary the name chosen for Windsor's new shopping centre, which was opened by Her Majesty the Queen on 8th April 1980 should be King Edward Court.

In addition to the Saturday markets, fairs were held in the town. In 1350 the Sheriff of Berkshire was ordered to cause two fairs to be held yearly at the town on the eve and feast of St George and two following days, and the eve and day of midsummer and three following days.

The Market House at that time was the one shown on Norden's plan which was built in 1596 and pulled down nearly a century later when the Guildhall was built on a site slightly to the north of it (1687-1690). The 'handsome Cross' was erected by John Sadler in 1380 at the meeting place of the town's four principal streets, near where the statue of Queen Victoria, erected in 1887, stands today. The market place had a 'common well'; there are references to it being repaired in 1518/19 and 1552 and in 1637-8 a new well was dug at the south end of the Market House. Near the well was the market bell which was re-hung in 1647. The pillory is mentioned in a 1658 lease as being the west boundary of a vault connected to a property now called Woods of Windsor. An order of 7th April 1691 required its removal 'for the more ornament of the town'. The five properties numbered 47-50 High Street, which extended from the south side of Castle Hill to Queen Charlotte Street, all had extensive vaults or cellars built under the road and the leases for the period 1658-1859 give their addresses as Market Place, not High Street. One lease dated 1735 stipulates that the surface over the vault is 'reserved to the mayor on public market and fair days'. The plan dated 1804 of the extensive vault attached to the corner property, now the Reject China Shop, marks 'wine cellar, coal hole and privy', and the vaults today form part of the basement sales display areas.

The river Thames was used from earliest times for the carriage of people and goods, and a road from the castle gate to the river must have been a very early development. It is thought that at first there was a ford across the river but this was replaced by a wooden bridge which FE Thacker dates as early as 1172. Although the river played an important part in the life of the town, the name Thames Street was not used until late in the eighteenth century. In the fourteenth and fifteenth centuries it was called Bisshopstrate and it has been suggested that the name came from Bishop's Tower, as the Salisbury Tower was called in the thirteenth century. The earliest known deed for a property in Bisshopstrate is dated 1312, and a group of fourteenth century leases for 'two messuages situated in Windsor in Underor under the castle in the street called Bysshoppe Street' shows that from an early date houses were built on the castle side of the street. Above the modern shop fronts the windows and rooflines reveal that there are still many old timber-framed buildings in Thames Street, and the Civic Trust award-winning development in Curfew Yard has exposed a little of medieval Windsor to view.

Eton College deeds indicate that Bisshopstrate was called Brig or Brigestrate in the sixteenth century and this certainly applied to a property

Thames Street in 1847 (RBMC) above and 2003 below (BM)

in lower Thames Street which extended from that street to River Street. However, the Manor House of Underore, which was later divided into two houses and which stood on the west side of the Hundred Steps, was leased by Windsor corporation for over two hundred years. The first lease dated 1639 locates it in the High Street but this changes in later leases to Thames Street. It seems probable that when Bisshopstrate changed its name in the sixteenth century the lower part was called Brigestrate and the rest High Street. Collier's map of 1742 marks the whole street Thames Street.

In the earliest known deed dated 1332 River Street is called Newestrate, and this suggests that it was built later than the other medieval streets in Windsor, probably to serve the developing goods wharf. By the sixteenth century its name had changed to Bereman Lane or Bereland and, as it is known that Andrew Symonds alias Bereman leased land adjoining the street, this is probably a reference to a brewery. Norden's plan of 1607 suggests a scattering of houses on each side of the street but this had become continuous development on the west side when Collier drew his map in 1742. Collier named the street Bear Lane but later the spelling changed to Bier Lane as shown on the 1791 plan of the houses in the castle ditch. The traditional explanation of this name is that because this part of Windsor was in the parish of Clewer, biers were taken along the street and causeway path for burial in Clewer churchyard. However, the lane is called Beer Lane in a painting dated 1880 and perhaps the rather innocuous name of River Street was adopted in 1883 to end the confusion over spelling.

Left: River Street in 2003 (BM)
Above: River Street before Windsor's first car park
was built there in 1926 (NMR)

The River - Windsor's Oldest Highway

Windsor riverside today shows little evidence of the once busy wharves which handled a constant flow of passengers and goods. Our knowledge of the process of development of the riverbank immediately above the bridge as the main goods wharf for the town has been greatly increased as a result of the 1987 excavations by Wessex Archaeology of Jennings Yard, the site of a recently demolished nineteenth century bonded warehouse on the corner of River Street and Thames Avenue. The excavations revealed that since medieval times there had been a wharf on this site which was used for the loading and unloading of goods. For most of the eighteenth century a wooden wharf projected into the river above the bridge and this was demolished when Neville Reid's wharf was built early in the nineteenth century. On this wharf barges discharged cargoes of coal which was the main upstream cargo, and loaded up with barrels of ale from the Windsor breweries. The volume of goods may be judged by a table of 1776 which shows a total of 98,670 tons of goods carried from London up river: 7,460 tons to Staines, 15,800 tons to Windsor, 5,560 tons to Maidenhead and 69,770 tons above Boulter's Lock.

There appears to have been very little development in the area known as Thameside before the seventeenth century and this may be due to the fact that it formed part of the manor of Underore and was in the ownership of the Abbot of Reading until 1539. In the seventeenth century the river was a fashionable means of passenger transport and there was a regular service of rowboats plying between Queenhithe (near St Paul's Cathedral) and Windsor. A 1731 lease refers to 'the rowbarge' which was apparently moored downstream from the bridge. Other surviving deeds refer to the king's slaughterhouse, which stood near the entrance to the engine river on the east side of the road which was later known as Little Datchet Lane, and to two tanyards near the river and a brewery in the site of the dean and canons' stable, are more suggestive of an early form of industrial estate than of residential development. However, houses were built there in the eighteenth century but most of these were swept away when, as a result of the Commissioners of Woods and Forests decision in 1849 to permit the extension of the South Western Railway line from Blackpotts to a point called Farmyard adjoining Datchet Lane, the Windsor and Eton Riverside station was built.

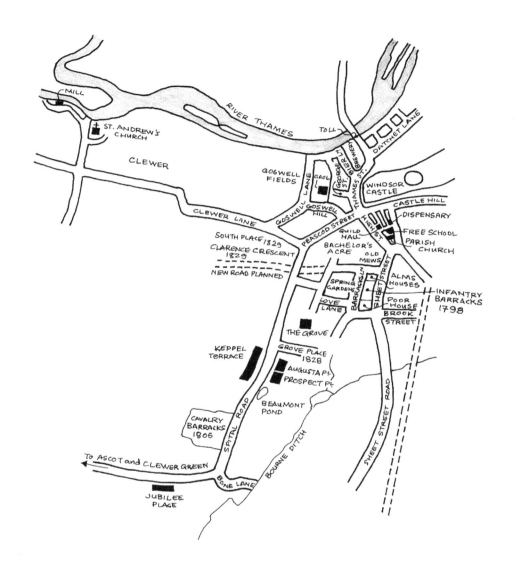

Windsor as it was between 1800 and 1829 (CG)

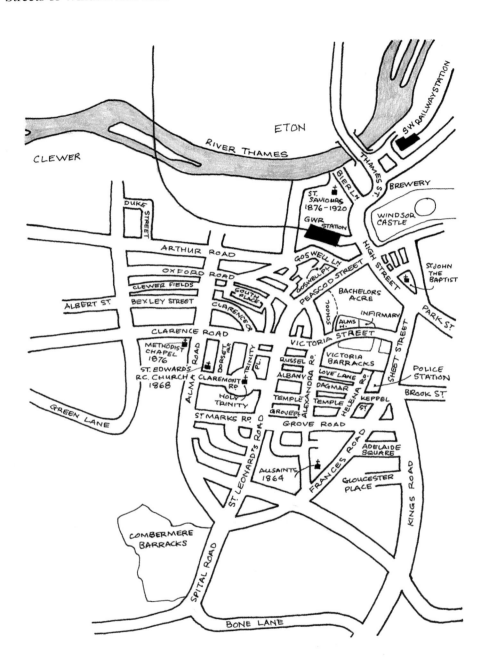

Windsor in 1880 (CG)

The ancient landscape

Beyond the confines of the little town were the fields of Windsor. Some no doubt were as ancient as the villages themselves, created when the Saxons or earlier people cleared the woodlands for tillage. However, from surviving records of the thirteenth century we can begin to get a detailed picture of the countryside. Then there were large fields, often surrounded by a hedge or fence, and divided into numerous unhedged strips or selions. The strips, owned by many different people, were arranged in groups called furlongs, which gave each field a chequerboard appearance. The Sheet is perhaps the oldest of the known field names for it is derived from a West Saxon word meaning a corner of woodland. It is first recorded in a deed from the reign of Henry III (1261-1272).

The Sheet lay immediately south of the town, stretching as far as the Bourne brook. High Field was probably south of the town, and presumably on higher ground as suggested by its name. It is unlikely to have been so far west as the road now called Highfield. The Sheet and High Field were mainly arable fields in contrast to the Goswells which was both arable and meadow. Its name means goose stream and presumably, the town geese were allowed to feed here. Of the other medieval names of fields and meadows only a few are commemorated in modern street names. Ray Mead was a meadow lying by the Thames north of Dedworth; it is now mainly covered by the racecourse which was laid out in 1865. It has been suggested that the name may be connected with the Ray family of Maidenhead, though no connection has been traced. It seems more likely from earlier spellings such as Reyemede that it comes from *rey* or *rei* meaning a stream; the meadows lie between the Thames and the millstream for Clewer Mill. South of the stream was West Mead, a meadow still divided into strips in the early nineteenth century. Upcroft is mentioned in deeds of 1295 and 1298; it too lay in Dedworth. Peascroft, however, another relatively small enclosed field or croft, lay close to the town of Windsor. It too was divided into strips, but used for growing peas, a valuable item in the diet of the people of the Middle Ages for peas could be dried and eaten in the winter when meat and fresh vegetables were scarce.

Peascod Street led to the croft as Sheet Street led to the field and Goswell Lane led to the meadow. These are ancient street names, but other medieval field names used today as street names – Highfield Road, Rays Avenue, Upcroft and Westmead – are the choice of modern planners.

Rye, a fast maturing cereal, was presumably grown in Rycroft and it is likely that Perrycroft was a pear orchard or that there was one adjacent. The *dunn* or Duncroft means either a small hill or indicates the colour brown. Ryding is a word, which combined with a name, is common in the records of Windsor Forest. It means a clearing taken in from the forest for cultivation, a process which took place from the earliest times until 1817 when the remaining parts of Windsor Forest were enclosed by Act of Parliament. All these names have been used in recent decades for the names of streets.

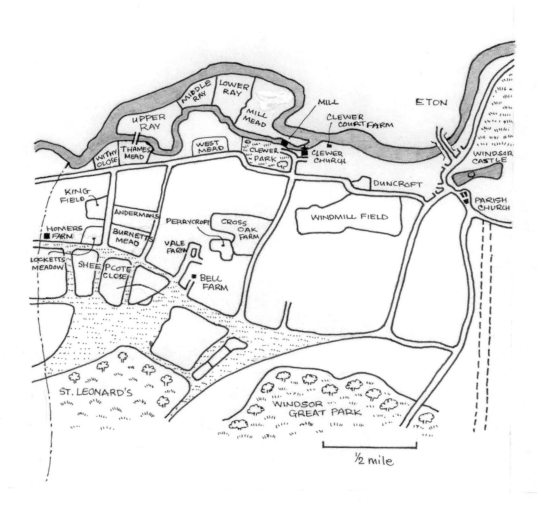

The road pattern in about 1800 showing the location of some
of the fields and parks used in street names (CG)

Maps of the eighteenth and nineteenth centuries have also been a rich source of names for modern streets, including many of those already mentioned, and they have the added advantage of showing us where the fields lay. A 1785 map of the parish of New Windsor includes the detached part of the parish known as the hamlet of Dedworth. This shows Andermans, Burnetts Mead, Duncroft, King Field, Locketts Meadow, Thames Mead, Upper, Middle and Lower Ray Meadow and West Mead, all of which were used as street names. It might be thought that King Field was once owned by the Crown; but in fact it belonged to William King from 1765, and to his widow after his death. Andermans and Burnetts Mead Meadow could have been similarly named though the latter name may have been descriptive of the burning process to which the field was once subjected. Withy Close is also shown, and no doubt it is to be associated with the growing of willow trees for the withies or willow stems which were used for making baskets, fish pots and eel traps. It was quite a common name and there was another Withy Close in the parish of Clewer.

An estate map of Arthur Vansittart of 1812 (a copy of a map a hundred years older) reveals the position of other fields now used as street names, such as Cross Oak, Perrycroft, Sheepcote Close and Meadow, Middle Riding and Windmill Field. Windmill Field was one of the largest surviving common fields, covering some forty-one acres and almost certainly taking its name from a windmill somewhere in the locality. Smock Acre in the north east corner of Windmill Field marks the site, if one assumes that smock refers to the type of windmill. A windmill is shown on the west side of the town on a seventeenth century engraving of Windsor by Hollar. The site of the windmill may also have been discovered some years back in what is now the north-east corner of the Vansittart recreation ground. Windmill Close, off nearby York Road may be named after this.

The Windmill shown on the West Side of Windsor in a drawing by Hollar c. 1600

In contrast there are many references to the watermill that stood to the north of Clewer village. The mill dates back to Saxon times for it is recorded in the Domesday Book and, although it has been rebuilt several times, it was still being used for grinding corn at the end of the nineteenth century. Mill Lane was the main street of the village and it still retains something of its earlier character.

Mill Lane today (PM)

The early maps of the countryside to the west of the town are too small scale to show street names. This had to wait for the inclosure maps of 1817 and 1819, on which Ash Lane, Blackhorse Lane, Datchet Lane, Hatch Lane, Roses Lane, Sherbourne Lane and Winkfield Road are shown and named. Roses Lane, today still an unmade road and half the length it once was, used to lead right down to the river where the reeds grew. One theory is that the name Roses derives from the Old French word for rushes or reeds which is *ros*. Sherbourne Lane became Smiths Lane and Ash Lane was renamed Sheepcote Road, while Blackhorse Lane no longer exists, though a new road was named Blackhorse Close but this was some distance from the old road. No doubt this road took its name from the nearby public house the Black Horse. Hatch Lane is an ancient road for it is part of the route connecting Clewer Village and Clewer Green. It is recorded in the Crown revenue accounts of 1548 as Woodhatch Lane and there is also mention of Woodhatch Gate. The word hatch comes from an Old English word meaning gate, often made of wattle, and it may not be too imaginative to assume that the gate closed off the lane from the green when livestock was pastured there.

Hatch Lane Clewer by the Convent of St John the Baptist in about 1930. (Photo G. Barnes. NMR)

The roads so far mentioned as shown on the Inclosure maps of New Windsor and Clewer were all old roads, but new roads were created by the Inclosure Commissioners. Most, like Clewer Green Road (later changed to Clewer Hill Road) followed the line of old tracks, though under the direction of the commissioners their route and width was properly defined. At least one road in Clewer, however, was entirely new. It was not given a name in the Inclosure Award, merely described as the first of the private roads. This is Green Lane, a straight road which once led out of the gently curving Hatch Lane, and perhaps will serve as an example of the planned landscape created by the Inclosure Act. These acts did away with the old commons, forest and open fields to make our familiar landscape of smaller hedged fields. One of the common meadows was Long Mead, a mile and a half from the road named after it.

Later maps of the nineteenth century point to an explanation of a small number of other street names such as Spinners Walk, named after Spinners Fields. More intriguing are the possible explanations for this name. Was it simply the name of a one-time owner? Or perhaps there is some truth in the tradition that it was associated with the scheme to help the poor in the seventeenth century by providing them with material for spinning. Lower and Upper Lammas Fields are shown on a large-scale map of the town of about 1860. *Lammas* was a Saxon word meaning loaf feast, a festival which celebrated the first fruits of the harvest. The lammas fields were usually common fields and meadows flung open for grazing after Lammas Day, 1st August, or when the harvest was gathered. By 1860 all lammas rights had been extinguished in Windsor, but the fields so named had once been part of the common field known as Hatton Hill and maybe centuries earlier as the Worth. There was a Lammas Lane, but the name was later given to a short cul-de-sac and a block of flats – Lammas Court.

The origins of another group of street names can be found from the earlier editions of the Ordnance Survey maps and local directories. The first edition of the 50 inch map shows Springfield House, which was named after a nearby spring. This has been known to flow in wet years within living memory, though it is now dried up as a result of drainage improvements. Grove Road got its name from Grove House which used to stand where Temple Road is now, but first there was Grove Place before the road was extended via Alexandra Road. Woodland Manor and Dedworth Manor, both relatively modern large houses with no manorial status, have apparently been used to name Little Woodlands, Woodland Avenue and Manor Road. On the other hand Mansell Close and Loring Road do commemorate real manors, divisions of the Domesday Manor of Dedworth. John Mauncell, lord of the manor, was mentioned in 1313 and a Peter Loring is recorded as holding land in Dedworth in the thirteenth century. Even when the manors became part of the Crown property the names persisted.

A number of farms were remembered in the names of streets. Clewer Court Farm has already been mentioned in a previous chapter; others include Bell Farm, Butler's Farm, Homer's Farm, Lovejoy Farm and Vale Farm. Bell Farm lay on the north side of Clewer Green. Whatever the original derivation of the name, people remember that early in the twentieth century a bell was used to call the workers. The farmland became a housing estate which was known during its development stage as Bell Farm Estate. Bell View and Bell View

Close were names given to roads on that estate. Manor Farm became a council housing estate and the names of many of the roads are old field-names such as Rydings, Rycroft and Perrycroft. However, these fields were some distance from Manor Farm. Poolman was the farmer who had Keeper's Farm, early in the twentieth century the farm was often simply known as Poolman's. In about 1948 the Borough's first old people's bungalows were built in Keeper's Farm Close.

Public houses and inns have long played an important role in the life of the community and it is not surprising to find some roads named after them. Wolf Lane is an old road, at least in part, and there has been a public house of that name in Dedworth since the early nineteenth century. It was more recently known as The Maypole but sadly it has now been demolished. Beaumont Road, built about 1901, took its name from the Beaumont pond which was drained in 1824 to widen St Leonard's Road, or perhaps from the Beaumont Arms, which stood at the junction of the road with St Leonard's Road. George Street, which was lost when the GWR station was built, took its name from the George Inn. This was one of the largest and most important inns in Windsor from the mid fifteenth century to the end of the seventeenth century. It stood on the castle side of Thames Street until the building was demolished with many others when the environs of the castle were improved in the 1850s.

The Wolf at Dedworth as it was on the day before it was demolished (PM)

One of the ancient elements of the Windsor landscape was the forest, a huge area of woodland, heath, marshy areas and parkland, over which the harsh laws of the forest prevailed. Little of the original woodland is now left, locally perhaps only High Standing Wood, which lies just south of Legoland, is all that remains. Few of the ancient descriptive names have survived and only one, Cranbourne, has been used as a street name. The name means the stream inhabited by cranes, and in the Middle Ages Cranbourne Chase was a privately owned part of the Royal Forest. It did not become part of the Great Park until the sixteenth century. The other street names which might be associated with the forest are disappointingly mundane – Wood Close, Forest Road, and those named after individual trees such as ash, birch, chestnut, copper beech, elm, fir, holly and oak. It is even difficult to be sure that the tree names are connected with the forest. Oak Lane was once Bexley Terrace and its newer name is much more likely to have been taken from Cross Oak Field which lay in the vicinity, or even the pub Herne's Oak which stood at the end of the street.

The Cranbourne stream marked the boundary between Clewer and Windsor for over two miles, from Cranbourne Chase almost into the town, where it was known as the Bourne. It once marked the southern limits of the town fields. Bourne Avenue was built within a few yards of the stream. Once the Bourne flowed through the fields of the former hamlet of Frogmore until it emptied itself into the Thames. It was later confined to the Crown sewer. Brook Street followed the line of a small brook, now culverted, which for much of the nineteenth century drained the Infantry Barracks. Then it was a dirty, stinking black ditch which bred death and disease. Most of the other streets named after waterways have been mentioned in the other chapters – River Street, Thameside and Thames Street – but the remaining two have rather more interesting meanings. Ruddlesway derived its name from Ruddlespool, first recorded in 1286 and described as lying on the parish boundary between Dedworth and Bray. It is similarly mentioned in the perambulation of Dedworth in 1801. Its name comes from the Old English *hrod* and means the reed pool, and it lay by the Thames. Bridgewater was also part of the Thames, though in this case it was the name of the great fishery of Windsor owned by the Corporation. One of the earliest leases reserves one draft of fish for the mayor. Salmon, eels and other fish were once abundant and a later lease even reserves swans for the mayor. The last Thames salmon was caught in Ruddlespool before the river became too polluted to support these fish. Salmon reappeared in the river after it was cleaned up.

This photograph of the barracks, taken in the 1970s, shows the old police station which became part of the barracks in 1916. It was formerly the workhouse and then the borough gaol. Before that it was the pest house given to the town by Thomas Alden. On the left is the extension to the barracks built in 1916 and on the right is the 1865 building. (BM)

Sheet Street in 2003 (BM)

The Great Park does not seem to have inspired any street names besides perhaps Park Street; Park Corner and Lodge Way would appear to take their names from the park on St Leonard's Hill which belonged to the house of the same name.

The final three names which might relevantly be considered in this chapter on the ancient landscape are very different in character. Hilltop was the inspiration of one member of the planning committee when ideas were waning. The site merely reminded him of a similar one in Kent! In contrast, Little Buntings was the choice of the developer. He wanted the name to remind him of the great number of these birds he thought were once seen in that area, though they are in fact very rare in this country. Lastly, Greenacre has a central green to give explanation to its name, but this is the site of a huge conical pit where clay was dug for brick making, so long ago it had faded from memory. During the Second World War a council dust destructor, positioned here, was hit by a VI flying bomb. A trial boring by the developers revealed that the old excavation pit had been completely filled with town refuse. Thus Greenacre represents two facets of the Windsor landscape now lost.

(PM)

Churches, chapels and schools

A Windsorian of the Middle Ages would have known only two streets in his town with names associated with churches. Church Lane adjoining the parish church in the High Street was then Church Street, and St Leonard's Road was for centuries known as Spittle or Spital Road, because it was the road that led to the leper hospital of St Peter. Today there are many more street names with church connections. Some were named after the new churches and schools as the town developed, and for the others the developers have looked back into history.

Royal Horse Guards marching to the Garrison Church along St Leonards Road, The Lord Raglan Public House is in the background. (BMc)

One stretch of the old road from Clewer Village to Clewer Green Village now called Parsonage Lane was previously Rectory Lane, and the house of the rector is shown on the earliest map of the area dated about 1762. A new rectory at 14 Parsonage Lane was left to the church, and the then rector of Clewer moved into it in about 1954. The old rectory was demolished in 1963 for the development of Chantry Close. This close was named after the Chantry Chapel in St Andrew's Church Clewer of Sir Bernard Brocas, who in 1384 obtained a licence to found and endow a chapel with land, the rent from which would support a priest to pray regularly for the soul of the benefactor. The close on the opposite side of Parsonage Lane was called Rectory Close.

Continuing south from Parsonage Lane is Hatch Lane and a group of streets associated with the convent of St John the Baptist. The sisterhood, which began in 1852 under the first mother superior Harriet Monsell, was primarily concerned with the rescuing of fallen women, though they also cared for the sick and poor of the parish. These women had previously been cared for by Mrs Mariquita Tennant, a clergyman's widow, at her home now The Limes, next to Clewer church, until ill health forced her to give up in 1851. As the convent of St John the Baptist grew in numbers, their work expanded into the slum area of Clewer Fields, and on 29th October 1868 St Stephen's Mission and temporary chapel was blessed by the rector the Rev T T Carter. The first stone of St Stephen's Church was laid on 9th November 1870, and on 25th July 1871 it was opened, although it was not to be completed and consecrated until December 1874, when it became a separate parish for people who

The altar of the Brocas Chapel in St Andrews Church Clewer (PM)

Windsor, St. Stephen's College and Church.

*St Stephens College and
Church (above) (BHc) and the
same view in 2003 (PM)*

lived in the small houses in the area. The name of Canon Carter, who as rector of Clewer did so much to help the initial work of the sisters, was commemorated in Carter Close and another clergyman, Canon Bailey, was remembered by Bailey Close. Both of these small roads were built off Hatch Lane, as also were Convent Road, St John's Road and St John's Drive, names derived from the convent, which has now been sold for housing development. Harriet Monsell is honoured in Monsell Walk opposite the convent.

St Andrew's Avenue and St Andrew's Crescent, both taking their name from the patron saint of Clewer parish church, were built after the sale of the Bell Farm estate. This had been acquired by Sir Daniel Gooch, the famous railway engineer and chairman of the GWR who lived at Clewer Park, but after his death it passed to members of his family, and in 1907 was purchased by agents for the convent of St John the Baptist. When in the 1930s the land was sold for development it is said that a stipulation was made that only bungalows be built, so that the convent was not overlooked!

Holy Trinity church was built on a part of Spinners Field, given by James Bedborough, a Windsor builder who was a prominent citizen, twice mayor of Windsor and member of the council for many years. No road in Windsor has yet been named after him. Holy Trinity was consecrated in 1844 to serve not only the needs of the growing population of this part of the town but also as a garrison church. Trinity Place was built from the church to Clarence Road, and Claremont Road was at first referred to as Church Road.

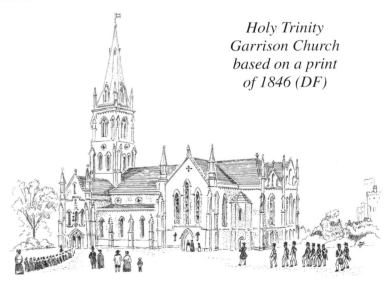

*Holy Trinity
Garrison Church
based on a print
of 1846 (DF)*

Near the church, behind the East Berkshire College, Hawtrey Road was named to commemorate the brothers Stephen and Henry Hawtrey who were the first two incumbents of that church.

Stephen Hawtrey, while still a master at Eton, was a curate at Windsor parish church and took a particular interest in the hamlet of Dedworth, then a detached portion of the parish of Windsor. He held services in a room or open field there, and from 1840 in St Leonard's School, which was at the corner of Tinkers Lane. Hawtrey took with him each Sunday some boys from the Free School, and later acquired a cottage in Clewer Lane in which to teach them. This school soon grew and was called St Mark's School, with Rev Robert Blyth and Mr Charles Morgan, one of the original Dedworth boys as masters. By 1861 it had outgrown these premises, and as it was held in such high esteem locally a subscription list was opened, headed by Queen Victoria, Prince Albert and the Duchess of Kent, to build a new school on land of the Vansittart estate in Alma Road. The school was opened on 25th April 1862 (St Mark's day). St Mark's Road and St Mark's Place remind us of this school.

The junior part of the school was in Grove Road, as signified by a plaque on the Parish Hall there. (DH)

In 1906 the school amalgamated with United Services College to become the Imperial Service College. In 1922 Clewer Manor House was purchased and became the junior school.

The name changed yet again in 1942 with the merger with Haileybury College and was known as Haileybury Junior School. The school having closed, the site has been re-developed in 2002 and named Longbourn. The houses are named Wickham House, Pemberley Lodge, Maryton House, Lambton House and Hunsford Lodge, all these names being drawn from Jane Austen's *Pride and Prejudice* and of no local significance whatsoever. However, nearby Haileybury Court and Imperial Court reminds us of the old associations. Imperial Road, named after the college, was built in 1923 on the line of the old footpath known locally as Lover's Walk, as unemployment relief work. College Crescent was built on land sold by the Imperial Service College. The original College site was very extensive, but was severed by Goslar Road. The school hall was built by subscription as a memorial to the King Edward Horse Regiment, but was demolished in the 1980s. Camperdown House and Kipling Building were school houses, the latter, with its memorial plaque to the writer depicting his jungle animals was used as council offices for many years, and was demolished in the 1980s to make way for commercial offices; today only Kipling Court reminds us of the old association.

St Leonards Road, looking towards Peascod Street (RBMC)

Spital Road or Street, named as we have seen after the medieval leper hospital which was situated on the corner of Spital Road and Bone Lane, was always one of the most important approaches into Windsor from the south, leading as it did to Peascod Street and the castle. Although the road was renamed in the latter part of the nineteenth century, the old name was preserved in the church of St Agnes Spital. The new name was St Leonard's Road. Later roads were called St Leonard's Avenue and St Leonard's Hill. St Leonard himself was a Frankish nobleman of the sixth century who became a hermit. His cult had become fashionable in the

Norman period, and it was probably at this time that the Windsor chapel and the hermitage of St Leonard was established in the forest. First mentioned in 1215 the chapel and hermitage continued until the dissolution of the monasteries in the sixteenth century and was undoubtedly a place of pilgrimage for many years.

In 1826 a house called Chapel House was built in Chapel Lane; it is called the Hermitage today and the lane is Hermitage Lane off St Leonard's Road. It contained the first local Roman Catholic chapel and school since the dissolution. In 1868 it was replaced by the church of St Edward the Confessor in Alma Road.

The same view of St Leonards Road in 2003. (BM)

The names of three roads in Dedworth, Abbots Walk, Monks Road, and Priors Road, help to perpetuate a legend that there was a priory or monastery here, although no documentary or archaeological evidence has ever been found to substantiate this, however, Church Terrace is aptly named behind All Saints Church. Bishop Selwyn, Primate of New Zealand and Bishop of Lichfield, who was curate to the Vicar of Windsor from 1833 to 1841, has given his name to a close off Dedworth Road. Rev Selwyn had a schoolroom built in Dedworth which became St.Leonard's School, on the site of what is now Deacon Court.

Rev. George Selwyn when he was Bishop of Lichfield

Sometimes the name of a road will come to have more than a single association. Thus although Tudor Way seems obviously linked with Stuart Way and Hanover Way and the royal families bearing these names, it was in fact named after the Rev Henry Tudor who was of some importance in Dedworth in the nineteenth century. He had been a curate of Canon Carter of Clewer, but when his wife Maria Sophia died, he and his children built the church of All Saints Dedworth to her memory in 1863. This became unsafe and was demolished in 1969, a new building opened in 1973. Somewhat in the same way, Redford Road may be named after the sixteenth century mayor of that name, but there was also a nineteenth century Congregational minister, Rev Alexander Redford. He came to the Congregational chapel in Bier Lane (River Street) in 1804, and by 1814 the membership became so large that the old Theatre Royal at 56 High Street, next to the parish church, was purchased and converted to a chapel. In May 1832 the foundation stone was laid for a splendid chapel in William Street and the Rev Redford continued as minister until his death in 1840 at the age of 81. This chapel was demolished in 1979 and the United Reformed Church, the lineal descendant of the Congregational Church, has a chapel in the new complex built on the site.

Behind this chapel another Congregationalist Joseph Chariott, endowed a charity for almshouses for the elderly, and he contributed both to this and to the building of the British School next door. He is believed to have come to Windsor as a young carpenter, and by much hard work became a builder and property developer. A delightful tale is told that Joseph Chariott did not trust banks and after his death in 1848, all his money was found in his house. It was loaded on to a cart, and on the way to the bank the bottom fell out with the weight. The pathway to the almshouses past the former British School (now demolished) was called Chariott's Place.

Chariotts Charity (CG)

A Clewer Rector, Roland Errington, 1880-1900, has had Errington Drive named after him. Ellison House, the former Almshouses in Victoria Street was named after Canon Henry John Ellison, Vicar of Windsor 1855-1862. Therefore Ellison Court may have been named after Henry John Joshua Ellison, Vicar of Windsor 1895-1913, or one of two famous surgeons in Windsor at that time, father and son, by the name of James and William Ellison. Terrent Court may commemorate another rector of Clewer, Jerameele Terrent, 1661-1677, but we have no proof of this. Dr Thomas Dawson was a long serving vicar of Windsor in the eighteenth century. He published *Memoirs of St George and the Order of the Garter*. There was also the Rev E Dawson-Walker, Rector of Holy Trinity Church. Dawson Close would have been named after one of these.

Among the changes in the centre of Windsor is the old Royal Free School on Bachelors Acre, which ceased to be an educational establishment during the 1980s. It is called simply Royal Free Court. Similarly the Infant School in Alexandra Road has become Alexandra Court, but the old St Anne's School, which later became Holy Trinity School, in Alma Road is now called Hunter's Mews. Another example of the developer naming a site for reasons unknown to us.

Trevelyan School, named after the Labour minister of education Sir Charles Trevelyan, who opened the school in 1930 on the corner of Imperial Road and Clarence Road has now been razed to the ground. The site is being developed for housing and will probably be called Trevelyan. The school has moved to the premises of the Princess Margaret Royal Free School in Bourne Avenue, the latter having been closed and the pupils dispersed to other schools in the Borough.

In common with most towns in the 18th and 19th centuries, wealthy citizens endowed charities for the poor and they are remembered in the following roads:

Ballard Green; Charles Ballard established Ballard's Charity in 1803. This charity paid for gifts of bread or cash to be given to twelve poor people of Windsor.

Franklyn Avenue; Henry Franklyn established a charity in the sixteenth century to help the poor of Windsor, Old Windsor and Clewer. Part of the income was from land in Clewer and part from a house in Park Street. In 1720 an almshouse was built on the Park Street site for twelve people and their present-day equivalents are now accommodated in Ellison House.

Kings, Queens and their relations

It is no surprise that Windsor has many street names relating to the kings and queens of England and a few of their near relations. Monarchs created Windsor Castle, and the citizens of the community associated with it celebrated them by calling new roads by their names. But this has largely been a modern phenomenon. When the town first developed below the castle walls the townspeople knew their streets by practical names which indicated their functions: Church Street, Fish Street, Butchers Row, Pound Street and so on. It is from the more sentimental nineteenth century that streets were given names honouring living royalty or reflecting Windsor's past royal connections.

Queen Charlotte Street (BM)

Queen Charlotte Street, the narrow passage that runs beside Market House and said to be the shortest street in the country, may be the first which was named after a royal figure. Queen Charlotte was the wife of George III; he had made Windsor his principal residence in 1778 and was a well-known and much-liked figure in the town until his disappearance from the public scene in 1810 following the onset of permanent derangement.

Nevertheless it is his wife who is commemorated by a place-name; she encouraged the establishment of a free dispensary for the town in 1817, and she patronised local tradespeople such as Mrs Maria Caley, who set up her first shop in 1815 and became the Queen's milliner. Caley's later developed into Windsor's foremost retailers.

George IV, Queen Charlotte's eldest son, made many changes to the local landscape, transforming the Castle's profile by raising the height of the Round Tower, overseeing developments around Virginia Water and commissioning the Copper Horse in his father's memory (his father would have been surprised since they did not get on well). But he was an unpopular monarch and nothing was named after him at the time; Regent Court off Sheet Street makes belated recognition. In 1828 George IV's brother, William Duke of Clarence and High Steward of Windsor (who became William IV), was honoured in the naming of Clarence Crescent. His wife Queen Adelaide, a kindly, popular woman, had Adelaide Square and Adelaide Terrace named after her. Nearby Gloucester Terrace is called after her royal friend Mary, Duchess of Gloucester; it is nice to think of the two old ladies still side by side. Mary, Duchess of Gloucester had been the most beautiful of George III's daughters and she lived longer than any of his children; when she died in 1857 she became the first member of the royal family to be brought back for burial in Windsor by train. Another of George III's sons, Frederick Duke of York, the original of the 'Grand old Duke' of the nursery rhyme, may have given his name to York Place off Sheet Street, though there have been many Dukes of York (there was no Duke of York when York Road was created in the early 1900s, but York Avenue built just before the Second World War may be named after George VI before he inherited the crown).

It was in Queen Victoria's reign that royal street-naming became commonplace. The Queen, like George III, made Windsor Castle her main residence (and honeymooned within its walls) but she felt ambivalently about it, writing in 1858 to her daughter Vicky, the Princess Royal, 'I long for our cheerful and unpalace-like rooms at Osborne and Balmoral'. Nevertheless there is a network of roads named after her and her immediate family in the town. The 'New Road' created in 1823 to go from Sheet Street to Dedworth, had become Victoria Street, Clarence Road and Dedworth Road by the 1850s. Queens Road off St Leonard's Road is another which got its name during her reign. Victoria's beloved husband Prince Albert gave his name to Albert Road between Windsor and Old Windsor. Albert was active in improvements and social welfare, and his interest in

Clarence Crescent above and Adelaide Square below(BM)

housing is reflected in the Prince Consort Cottages. A 'Royal Association for Improving the Conditions of Labourers' was set up after the Great Exhibition of 1851 which Albert had master-minded, and the Windsor cottages, designed for 'well-conducted families of the labouring classes' were built as a result. Good sanitary conditions were an important feature of their building, at a time when many died of typhoid and cholera. Albert Street in Clewer was built and named after his death in 1861.

Prince Consort Cottages (VS)

Windsor Roads and Windsor Streets dating from Victorian times are a feature of many English towns, and in Windsor itself two of Victoria's other residences are commemorated in Osborne Road, Osborne Mews, and Balmoral Gardens. Claremont Road was named after Claremont near Esher in Surrey, where Victoria had spent time in her childhood and which became the home of her youngest son, Leopold, Duke of Albany. He suffered from haemophilia and died young, but in 1878 had encouraged the formation of the Royal Windsor Tapestry Manufactory in Old Windsor, where the Tapestry Hall built for the weavers can still be seen. Prince Leopold also gave his name to Albany Road.

Victoria's third son, Arthur Duke of Connaught, is remembered in Arthur Road, and her daughter Helena, who married the penniless Prince Christian of Schleswig-Holstein, is commemorated in Helena Road. The couple were given Cumberland Lodge to live in and he was found a role by being made Ranger of Windsor Great Park and High Steward of Windsor. Princess Helena was deeply committed to nursing and established the Princess Christian Nursing Home in the town. It was probably after her son Christian Victor, who was killed in the Boer War, that Victor Road was named, rather than Albert Victor, eldest son of Edward and Alexandra.

The beautiful Princess, later Queen, Alexandra, daughter of Christian IX of Denmark, who married the Prince in 1863, was always admired in Windsor, and Alexandra Road was named after her. Dagmar Road remembers her sister who married Alexander III of Russia and became mother of the ill-fated Tsar Nicholas II, murdered by the Bolsheviks. Edward VII is commemorated in King Edward VII Avenue and in the Edward VII Gateway. This, according to a plaque erected in December 1997, was a gift to the 'citizens of Windsor by Sir Jesse Boot and opened by Princess Alice, Countess of Athlone in January 1921'; Boots Passage led from Thames Street down to Alexandra Gardens, but Boots the Chemists has long since moved its premises into Peascod Street.

Victoria Street in 2003 (BM)

*Charles Street before the cottages were demolished in the
1940s (above) (RBMC) and in 2003 (below) (BM)*

Later twentieth-century monarchy has been remembered, most obviously in Ward Royal. In this post-war complex can be found Christian Square for Princess Christian, and Athlone Square named after Princess Alice, daughter of Prince Leopold. Bowes-Lyon Close records the maiden name of Queen Elizabeth the late Queen Mother who had been Lady Elizabeth Bowes-Lyons. Mountbatten Square is named after Prince Philip who was Lieutenant Philip Mountbatten when he married the present Queen. Charles House commemorates their eldest son, the present High Steward of Windsor. Princess Avenue was named after Princess Elizabeth when she received the freedom of the borough in 1947, and Edinburgh Gardens after the Duke of Edinburgh. It is surprising that no development has been given the name Elizabeth, but Station Approach has been renamed Jubilee Arch following the Golden Jubilee of 2002. Wessex Court (off Russell Street) recognises Prince Edward, Earl of Wessex.

In the post-war developments of West Windsor names with royal associations of earlier times were used. Although Tudor Way commemorates the Rev Henry Tudor who built All Saints Church Dedworth rather than the Tudor dynasty, the name sits well alongside Stuart Way and Stuart Close, Hanover Way and Hanover Close which do reflect past history. James Street (off Victoria Street) and Charles Street (off Clarence Road) are perhaps named after the Stuart kings. James I hunted enthusiastically in the Great Park and King Charles I spent the last days of his life before trial and execution in the Castle.

> There is no street-name memorial for the king-breaker, Oliver Cromwell, even though the town was for Parliament in the Civil War.

The so-called merry monarch Charles II created the Long Walk and oversaw various improvements to the Castle, but his brother, James II, was forced to abdicate after only three years.

Queen Anne's contribution to Windsor has been recognised in Queen Anne's Road and Queen Anne's Court (off Peascod Street). She was another enthusiast for hunting, with a specially-designed one-seater hunting chariot which she drove furiously through the Park. She created Queen Anne's Ride, and surfaced the Long Walk to give her chariot easier passage. But she gave thought to the town too, heading the list of subscribers for a charity school for 70 poor children, the Royal Free School. Her statue, and that of her husband Prince George, are seen on the Guildhall, but they had no surviving children despite seventeen pregnancies and the Hanoverian kings succeeded, though it was not until the reign of George III that any of them took any interest in Windsor.

Finally there is Kings Road. Its name is first found in the seventeenth century but seems never to have been associated with any particular king. But as a road which all kings might use to make their way to the Castle it seems well-named for the monarchy in general, and for all of us who claim the right to walk upon and enjoy the king's, or queen's, highways.

(PM)

Tinker, tailor, soldier...

Tinker: There is a Tinkers Lane in Windsor and although there have been Tinkers in the town: Isaac and Thomas Tinker are mentioned in seventeenth century records, it is more likely that Tinkers Lane was named after the tinkers or pedlars who used this ancient way through the forest.

Tinker *Tailor*: Many of Windsor's leading citizens were occupied with trades in food and drink, building and services and the manufacture of clothes. They served not only the town but also the court and the garrison. These leading citizens had never been commemorated, it is only recently that the practice has grown up of attaching the names of prominent citizens to new streets. Private developers can, within wide limits, pursue their own policy when choosing names for new estates, although they have to be approved by the council. The names they choose may have significance to *them* but none to the town of which the streets form a part. The chief exception has been Messrs Laing, whose large private housing estate in West Windsor added some 1,000 new houses to the town between 1960 and 1965. Here many of the streets were named after prominent citizens included in the list prepared by the council. Many of these are Mayors from earlier centuries, and it is perhaps worth making the comment that, when they lived, Windsor was a small town clustered round the walls of the castle and the streets named after them were away in the countryside and not even in Windsor then. The streets named after these earlier Mayors are:

Whiteley	Thomas 1495, 1497; John 1560, 1568
Gwynne Close	Matthew 1539, 1545, 1548; William 1586, 1587
Hylle Close	Gabriel 1558
Hanley Close	William 1559
Gallys Road	Richard 1561, 1566, 1570
Redford Road	Richard 1573, 1583
Jacob Close	William 1575
Aston Mead	Thomas 1580
Needham Close	Richard 1582, 1583
Clifton Rise	Thomas 1584
Bradshaw Close	Robert 1586
Alden View	Thomas 1592, 1597, 1605
Washington Drive	Richard 1596, 1600, 1613, 1606, 1613

Frymley View	John 1594
Hayse Hill	Thomas 1599
Cawcott Drive	Robert 1601
Fawcett Road	Humphrey 1602, 1607, 1615

Most of these were on or adjoining the Laing Estate as well as Newberry Crescent named after Humphrey Newberry who was Recorder 1608-13 and 1624-38. A sprinkling of streets on other new estates and elsewhere in Windsor were named after later mayors, such as:

Merwin Way	Thomas 1669, 1681
Bridgman Drive	James 1687
Gilman Crescent	Samuel 1697, 1705, 1718, 1726
Snowden Close	John 1735, 1747, 1753, 1757; John 1800, 1812; Charles 1832, 1838
Bryer Place	Thomas Bryer 1732
Rowland Close	Thomas 1736
Benning Close	John 1765, 1775
Tyrell Gardens	William 1766, 1776
Knights Close	Charles Knight 1806, 1817
Leigh Square	possibly William Legh 1834, 1835
Devereux Road	Sir Joseph, 1869, 1881, 1882
Dyson Close	Thomas, 1890; Sir Frederick, 1909, 1910, 1922; Sir Cyril 1952, 1953
Luff Close	Thos. Edmund, 1912

Windsor in these earlier days was smaller than most modern villages. Even so the Mayors were civic dignitaries of importance in the local community and their names occur in leases, wills, by-laws, parish registers, municipal accounts and other early records. One man to whom we owe a great deal of our knowledge is Elias Ashmole, the seventeenth century antiquary who wrote *The Institutions, Laws and Ceremonies of the Most Noble Order of the Garter*, published in 1672. He transcribed many of the early records of the borough and, although the originals are now lost, his transcripts have been preserved in the Bodleian Library.

Only a few of these early Mayors emerge as distinct personalities. One who does is Richard Gallys. He was landlord of the Garter Inn, immortalised in Shakespeare's *Merry Wives of Windsor.* As well as being Mayor three times, he also represented Windsor in the House of Commons in Elizabeth I's reign and in his maiden speech in 1563 was bold enough to urge the Queen to marry.

Thomas Alden (or Aldem) was also Mayor three times. He gave to the corporation in 1604 a plot of land in Sheet Street. Here a pest house was built, which served as a refuge for the next hundred years for those afflicted with the plague or other infectious diseases. From 1769 to 1843 the building was used as a workhouse. Between 1845 and 1854 it served as the borough gaol, and until 1902 it was the Windsor police station, In 1916 the site became part of Victoria Barracks. When the old workhouse was sold, the proceeds were invested. The interest and dividends were used to establish four beds – known as Aldem beds – in the Windsor Royal Infirmary in Victoria Street.

We know more about some of the later Mayors. Snowden Close was named after a family which supplied Windsor with Mayors for several generations. The family had a grocery business in Peascod Street above Goswell Hill and Charles Snowden took a leading part in the 1840s in bringing the Great Western branch railway from Slough to Windsor – the station was right at the back of his shop.

Knights Close and Place recall the two Charles Knights, father and son, who founded the *Windsor and Eton Express* in 1812. Charles Knight senior was Mayor in 1806 and 1817; among his publications were some of the earliest guides to Windsor. His son also served on the council for a time but his activities took him away from Windsor and it was in London that he earned his fame as one of the most prominent popular educators of the nineteenth century. From 1828 to 1846 he superintended the publications of the *Society for the Diffusion of Useful Knowledge* as well as publishing popular editions of Shakespeare and reference books, such as the *Penny Cyclopaedia*. His three-volume autobiography, *Passages of a Working Life* published in 1864-5, contains many reminiscences of Windsor in the days of his youth.

Almost all the streets named after Mayors are post-war roads. Devereux Road is an exception for it was named after Sir Joseph Devereux – who was knighted by Queen Victoria in 1881 - when it was constructed in 1888.

The Dyson family also served Windsor for several generations and Dyson Close preserves their name. Thomas Dyson, a Yorkshireman, founded the business of Dyson & Sons, pianoforte dealers in Thames Street in 1865 and he eventually became Mayor in 1890. He was especially active in promoting improvements in the town, particularly in the riverside area as the drinking fountain erected in 1908 testified. His second son, Charles

Frederick Dyson, continued his activity in this field. Mayor in 1909 and 1910, he was knighted in King George V's coronation year, 1911. His nephew, Cyril Dyson, received a similar honour when he was Mayor at the time of Queen Elizabeth II's state entry to Windsor in 1953.

Thomas Edmund Luff, after whom Luff Close was named, was Mayor in 1912 and was a leading citizen in the town for many years, championing liberal causes as well as spending many years in collecting material for a history of Windsor. Throughout his career in Windsor he was associated with the printing and stationery business.

Other more recent Mayors who have been commemorated are:

Carey Close	Mrs Carteret Carey, 1937-39, Windsor's first woman Mayor
Fuzzens Walk	Frederick, 1937-39, Windsor's first Labour Mayor
Tozer Walk	Richard, 1949-52
Burton Way	Frank, 1961, 1971
Basford Way	Harold, 1962
Dean Close	Jack, 1967
Keeler Close	John D, (but always known as Ian) 1969

Several other members of the council with a special concern for housing have also been remembered: Allkins Close, Peter Allkins Royal Borough housing manager; Gratton Drive, Mrs A M Gratton, Borough and County Councillor; Kimber Close, Councillor Don Kimber; Wells Close, Councillor Harry Wells 1973-80; Proctor House, John Proctor, Mayor 1958-60 and 1973; also Churcher House, Leslie Dunne House, Jarratt House and the recently demolished Gray Court.

Only a few of Windsor's MPs appear in the street names. R Richardson-Gardner's name – he was MP from 1874 to 1890 – appears in Gardners Cottages in Vansittart Road / Duke Street. He became the landlord of several hundred working class houses in this area. It was said that the one condition he imposed on his tenants was that they should vote Conservative and those who voted against him in 1868, when he was defeated by a narrow margin in the last open general election, were evicted from their homes.

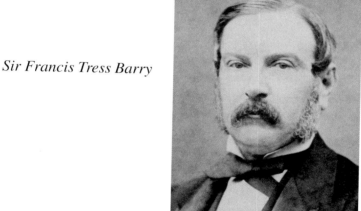

Sir Francis Tress Barry

His successor as MP was Sir Francis Tress Barry (MP 1890-1906). Born in 1825, he had in the course of a distinguished career held many posts, including that of Consul General to Ecuador. He resided in Windsor at St Leonard's Hill and was a staunch supporter of the Infirmary, of which he became chairman. In 1889 he gave £1,000 (one of many munificent donations) to establish an accident ward which became known as Barry Ward. It was in 1905 that Barry Avenue, the riverside promenade was constructed. It approximately followed the line of the path from the town to Clewer Church.

One MP who should have been commemorated is John Ramsbottom, a local banker and brewer, who was MP for Windsor from 1810-1845. As a tradesman he was looked down upon in Parliament and Wellington said of him 'We should be sorry to see the House of Commons composed of Ramsbottoms – that gentleman is a brewer in Windsor'.

There is a scattering of names of men with a special importance and interest in the history of Windsor. The earliest of these are those of the Windsor martyrs of 1544: Henry Filmer, Anthony Pierson and Robert Testwood, commemorated in Filmer Road, Pierson Road and Testwood Road. Associated with them is John Marbeck, the organist of St George's Chapel who escaped the fate of the others and lived to tell their story. Marbeck Close was named after him.

The Windsor Martyrs as they were burnt at the stake from the woodcut in Foxe's Book of Martyrs (CG)

Addington Close may be named after one of George III's physicians, although there was also Henry Addington, Viscount Sidmouth, Prime Minister from 1801-4. The sale of hospital land during the 1990s which included the former nurses' homes, allowed a new housing development which was called Nightingale Walk, no doubt after the famous nurse, Florence Nightingale. The road leading towards the new entrance of the hospital is called Sinclair Road commemorating Miss Gladys Doreen Sinclair-Brown, matron of King Edward VII hospital from 1953 to1972.

Camm Avenue and Camm House in Albert Street were named after Sir Sydney Camm (1893-1966), one of Windsor's most distinguished twentieth century sons. Educated at the Royal Free School, he became passionately interested in aeronautical engineering while he was still in his teens. A plaque in Ward Royal records that 'in a building on this site Sydney Camm designed and built his first powered aircraft in 1911/1912'. He was especially famous for his development on the Hurricane fighter plane which in 1940 played a significant part in the Battle of Britain. His services to the aviation industry were rewarded by a knighthood in 1953. A plaque on the house where he was born in Alma Road has been stolen twice.

Sir Sydney Camm
(WSEE)

It is natural that the names of landowners and their relations should be commemorated in street names. Bolton Road, Bolton Avenue and Bolton Crescent, for example, took their names form TD Bolton, a London man who bought the former Bourne estate with its old brickfields and developed the streets named after him. Smith's Lane was named after Henry Smith, a nineteenth century landowner in the Dedworth area. It is interesting to read that there was a Smythislane in the fifteenth century, as a deed of the time of Henry VI refers to a property in the parish of Clewer abutting on a lane of that name. But the honoured name of Smith was no doubt as common in the fifteenth century as in the nineteenth.

Keppel Street commemorates Frederick Walpole Keppel, who sold to the Commissioners of Woods and Forest in 1842 a large area of land on either side of the Long Walk. One consequence was that the Crown was able to join the Home Park with the Great Park. But it also made possible the building of new houses and the making of new streets to the west of the Long Walk.

Two distinguished families who are commemorated in the names of Windsor streets are Harcourt and Vansittart. Field-Marshal William, third Earl Harcourt (1743-1830), purchased St. Leonard's Hill about 1782 and with his countess played a prominent part in the affairs of Windsor for many years. On terms of intimacy with the royal family, he was Deputy Lieutenant of Windsor Castle, Deputy Ranger of the Great Park and in 1818 became the first President of the Windsor General Dispensary. He gained a reputation for his many generous benefactions, so it is fitting that there should be a Harcourt Road.

The Vansittart family held lands not only at Windsor but also at Bisham and Shottesbrooke. Arthur Vansittart, (1691-1760) whose family came from Sittart in Holland bought the Manor of Clewer in 1718. Robert Vansittart (1728-89) was the recorder of Windsor from 1772 until his death. With his brothers Arthur and Henry he was a member of the notorious Hell-Fire Club of Medmenham. Henry was the father of the most famous member of the family, Nicholas Vansittart (1766-1851), who was Chancellor of the Exchequer in Lord Liverpool's Government at the end of the Napoleonic Wars. In 1823 he became Lord Bexley; hence the two names of Vansittart Road and Bexley Street. Stovell Road also comes into the story, for another member of the family, Arthur Vansittart, left his Clewer Manor lands on his death in 1859 to Arthur and Gerald Stovell, his illegitimate sons by Rebecca Stovell. It is not clear if Arthur Road was named after the Vansittart Arthurs or Arthur Duke of Connaught. The public house called The Duke of Connaught in Arthur Road somewhat clouds the issue.

Bulkeley Avenue is named after Captain Thomas Bulkeley, who lived in Clewer Lodge. He was another landowner who played an important part in the affairs of the town. As chairman of the Great Western Railway Company (Windsor to Slough), he fought to bring the railway into the centre of Windsor. He was at length rewarded in 1849 when the central station was erected on the site of the notorious slum area of George Street. 'There cannot be a worse street in any town of England', he said of it.

Other streets which commemorate the names of landowners include Sherbourne Drive, after Henry Sherbourne, farmer and landowner, and Foster

Arthur Road from the multi-storey carpark at King Edward Court in the 1980s (PM)

Avenue - Squire Foster lived at Clewer Manor. A more recent street Martin Close, was named after Martin Laing, second son of the developer of the West Windsor estate.

Street names like Gordon Road and Nelson Road occur in many town because Gordon and Nelson were famous Englishmen, not because they had any local associations. However, it is interesting to know that the Lord Nelson who was a great-nephew of the Admiral, was a member of the committee formed for the purpose of presenting Canon Carter with a house of residence as warden of the Convent in Hatch Lane after he resigned his cure at Clewer in 1880. The name Nelson was given to a road within a short distance of the Convent.

Reverend Thomas Thellusson Carter 1808-1901 (PM)

Peel Close was appropriately named after Sir Robert Peel, founder of the Metropolitan Police, because this was the first post-1945 housing estate intended primarily for the police.

Tinker, tailor, *soldier*...The presence of the army in Windsor could hardly have failed to make itself felt. Combermere Close was obviously so named because of Combermere Barracks, but these in turn were named in honour of Viscount Combermere, Wellington's comrade-in-arms. One of Windsor's most important streets, Alma Road, was formed in the 1850s at the time of the Crimean War and named from the Battle of Alma, fought on 20 September 1854 to the north of Sebastopol. Then there are Cavalry Crescent and Barrack Lane – the latter so named because it was originally the lane behind the Infantry Barracks. When the barracks were extended westwards in 1865-67, it was blocked off, and thus became a *cul-de-sac* south of Victoria Street.

During the early 1970s the Broom Farm Estate to the west of Windsor was developed to provide married quarters for soldiers' families stationed in Combermere and Victoria barracks. The road names were chosen by the army; they commemorate guardsmen who were awarded the Victoria Cross during World War II. Leading from Guards Road are:

Charlton	Guardsman Edward Charlton, 2nd Battalion Irish Guards. VC 1945 Wistedt, Germany.
Furness	Lieutenant The Hon Christopher Furness, 1st Battalion Welsh Guards. VC May 1940 Arras, France.
Kenneally	Lance Corporal (later Company Quartermaster Sergeant) John Kenneally, Irish Guards. VC April 1943 Dj Bou Arada, Tunisia.
Liddell	Captain Ian Liddell, 5th Battalion Coldstream Guards. VC April 1945 Lingen, Germany.
Lyell	Captain The Lord Charles Lyell, 1st Battalion Scots Guards. VC April 1943 Dj Bou Arada, Tunisia.
Nicholls	Lance Corporal Harry Nicholls, 3rd Battalion Grenadier Guards. VC May 1940 near River Escaut, Belgium.
Sidney	Major William Sidney (later Viscount de L'isle), 5th Battalion Grenadier Guards. VC February 1944 Anzio, Italy.
Wright	Company Sergeant Major Peter Wright, 3rd Battalion Coldstream Guards. VC September 1943 Salerno, Italy.

And finally, not a spy but a hero. Winton House in Dedworth Road was named in honour of Sir Nicholas Winton who saved the lives of nearly 600 children when he arranged for them to escape from Czechoslovakia immediately before the Second World War.

Soldiers marching on the streets of Windsor.
Above the 1st Coldstream Guards in Victoria Street marching from their barracks,(BMc) and below Foot Guards marching in Sheet Street in 2003. (BM)

The Lost Streets and Street Names of Windsor

Over the centuries many Windsor street names have come and gone, either because streets were lost through re-development or they were re-named. The establishment of the Home or Little Park during the Middle Ages absorbed much of the manor of Underore to the north of the castle, and with it Back Lane and Little Lane. Later enlargements by William III at the end of the seventeenth century did away with other roads such as Poke (Goblin) Lane, used (according to *The Merry Wives of Windsor*) by John and Robert to take Falstaff in the basket of Mistress Ford's dirty linen to Datchet Mead for washing in the Thames.

The street pattern established at that time and shown on Norden's Map of 1607 remained almost unchanged through to the early nineteenth century. Collier's Plan of 1742 adds more houses and a number of lanes leading off Peascod Street. This plan also shows for the first time some of the street names in use at that time. Park Street was then called Pound Street, because this is where the pound or lock-up was, but it had also been known as Moor Street, because it led to the hamlet of Frogmore. From Castle Hill one could follow the road past the castle along Park Hill past Herne's Oak and over Dodds Hill towards the Datchet bridge which had been constructed in 1706. This 'Foot Way to Datchet' was closed during the early 1820s to give the royal family more privacy. Another way to get to Datchet was along the Datchet Lane, which followed the line of the river Thames to the Datchet bridge.

Datchet Lane was re-aligned in 1851, as part of an agreement with Queen Victoria to bring the South Western Railway into Windsor. The new road to Datchet, today called King Edward VII Avenue, crossed the Thames via the newly built Victoria Bridge. At the same time the old Datchet bridge was dismantled. Part of Datchet Lane was probably once called Mill Lane, because it led to the ancient town mill at Romney. Today this part of the old Datchet Lane is called Romney Lock Road. Another casualty of the deal with Queen Victoria was the Frogmore Road which used to lead from Park Street, and on to Old Windsor, Staines and London. It was replaced in 1851 by a new road further south called Albert Road, the so-called improvement road which formed a ring road encircling the castle and crossing the Thames towards Datchet by the Albert Bridge. Shoots Road, leading from the Long Walk to the former Hope public house in Frogmore became a private park road.

These old roads through the Little Park are clearly shown on Collier's map of 1742. At the Old Windsor end of the Frogmore Road was Gallows Lane with its grisly implications, but nothing is known today about this lane.

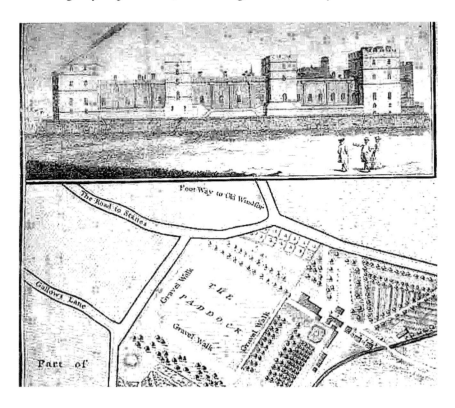

Section of Collier's Map of 1742 showing Gallows Lane

The Great Western Railway demolished George Street in 1849 to make way for Station Approach, which was re-named Jubilee Arch after the Golden Jubilee of Elizabeth II. Few people bemoaned the loss of George Street, being one of the most notorious quarters of the town, at the end of which stood the Windsor gaol.

The building of the two barracks in Windsor at the beginning of the nineteenth century and in particular the extensions of the Infantry Barracks in 1865-67 and again in 1916, resulted in the loss of a number of streets. In 1865 Spring Gardens disappeared, and most of Barrack Lane, leaving only a short cul-de-sac from Victoria Street. In 1916 Love Lane was extinguished by Act of Parliament, together with Braggs Yard, West Row and Wellington Square. No housing was provided for the people who lost their homes.

During the 1890s Keppel Terrace on St Leonard's Road was pulled down to make way for the new police and fire station. When a new police station was built in Alma Road and a new fire station in St Mark's Road, their old building became the Windsor Arts Centre. Keppel Terrace had been a row of beautiful Georgian houses similar to those of Grove Place, and there is no explanation for their destruction.

River Street, showing the brewery chimney. (RBWM)

The first major slum clearance of the twentieth century was in the River Street area in 1926. River Street itself was once Bereman Lane, Bear Lane and Bier Lane. It lay within Clewer and tradition is that its name originated from carrying biers down this street to the funeral services at Clewer Church. The streets and lanes behind River Street which disappeared had colourful names such as Red Lion Row, Garden Court, Providence Place and Distill House Row. They became Windsor's first car park. The houses in these streets lacked proper drainage and possessed an inadequate water supply – one tap to 23 houses, noted Dr Bulstrode in his report of 1900. Queen Victoria read this with horror and caused her private secretary to write to the mayor expressing her concern for the poor people living there. This resulted in members of the council visiting the houses and some were shocked enough to order steps to be taken against the owners. The Bench, however, did not make the necessary orders and little was done for another twenty years. The west side of the area included another Mill Lane, which led to a short-lived watermill just above Windsor Bridge in the seventeenth century. The line of this road was retained for the entrance to the car park.

Charles Street was a narrow lane running from Clarence Road in a large arc which followed the curve of Clarence Crescent, between South Place and Oxford Road to Alma Road. The last section near Alma Road was known as Clarence Clump. The first 28 cottages in Charles Street had been cleared by the late 1930s, becoming first a temporary car park. The car park was changed on Saturdays to the charter market when this was moved from the Guildhall area. Charles Street, which had only been about eight feet wide, was widened and straightened to become the new distribution road from Arthur Road, across Oxford Road East to Clarence Road during the 1970s. The Saturday market was moved to Bachelors Acre, but it has now disappeared altogether. The Clarence Clump part of Charles Street did not disappear until Ward Royal was built.

Modern engineering works such as the Relief Road caused the loss of the original Stovell Road, which disappeared under the incline up to the Thames bridge built in 1966. The name was then applied to that section of

Oxford Road when it was flooded in 1947 (GTc)

what was Barry Avenue west of its junction with Vansittart Road, along by the War Memorial Swimming Baths. The latter was replaced by a leisure pool in 1986.

Redevelopment schemes over the years have been built over old roads, but never before in Windsor on the scale of Ward Royal and King Edward Court during the 1960s. This obliterated the Victorian streets and lanes built in the Goswell flood plains. Under Ward Royal lie Denmark Street, part of Goswell Road, Grosvenor Place, South Place, part of Charles Street and Clarence Clump with Alma Cottages, as well as part of Oxford Road and some houses in Arthur Road. The development of King Edward Court during the 1970s obliterated Edward Square, Sydney Place, Goswell Place and part of Goswell Lane.

Some street names found in old records have just disappeared without trace, sometimes without their exact locations being known. These include the fourteenth century Gropencourt Lane, which was somewhere near the parish churchyard. The name gives an indication that there was a seedy and perhaps sinister part to the town. Alfred Mews, running from Clarence Road to Spinners Walk is a private car park now. An old name which can still be traced is Leworth Place, on the gables of the former Hull's workshop behind Peascod Street. It is now called Mellor Walk which can be reached via Peascod Place, once known as Sun Passage. Doris Mellor fought and won to save nearby Bachelors Acre

Oxford Road in 2003 (BM)

81

from becoming a car park in the 1970s. Keppel Row along Sun Passage has disappeared. Nearby Acre Passage is still there but gone are Myra- Gothic- and Hibberts Cottages.

Sometimes the Borough Council decided to rename a street to avoid postal confusion and loss of time in an emergency. One example is St Andrew's Road which was renamed and numbered as an extension of Duke Street in the 1950s to distinguish it from the other two St Andrew's – Avenue and Crescent on the Bell Farm Estate. Bexley Terrace was re-named Oak Lane to avoid confusion with Bexley Street.

The list of names that have changed over the centuries is a long one. Several such as Fish Street or Priest Street have been mentioned in other chapters. Gospell Lane off Russell Street has long been known as Garfield Place. Russell Street used to be called Chancery Lane; as it was renamed during the 1850s it is likely that it was called after Lord John Russell who was Prime Minister from 1846-1852. Mechanics Court off Thames Street became Curfew Yard. Victoria Lane became part of Victoria Street which had been part of New Road. Alexandra Road was first called Brewer Street, because of the brewery, replaced today by the Victoria Street car park, although part of the former brewery is still in Russell Street. Others include Bolton Road, which was known as Bone Lane from the Spital Bourne which it crosses. Clewer Fields, the old path to Clewer and Dedworth above the winter flood line, was once called Church Path, because it led to the church at Clewer. New Road was the name first used for Victoria Street, Clarence Road and Dedworth Road. Racecourse Road was once part of the road to Surly Hall and Maidenhead, the straight frontage of the racecourse to Maidenhead Road being a late nineteenth century re-alignment. The bank of the old road line held back the 1947 Thames flood for a while as this spread southwards towards Vale Road. Spital Road became St Leonard's Road and Clewer Lane became Oxford Road.

Finally, mention should be made of the several locations which have had nicknames. Goswell Hill with its granite sets to assist horses to get a grip with their hooves when pulling carts up to Peascod Street was called Break-Neck Alley. Alexandra Road was once referred to by locals as Gun Street Avenue because the territorial soldiers kept their howitzer there, by St Leonard's Avenue. Sydney Place, which used to lead from Peascod Street to the Methodist church, was known as Creak's Passage because William Creak Ltd dominated this part of Peascod Street until the 1950s with a number of outfitters and furniture shops on both sides of the street. Zigzag cottages in Goswell Lane received their nickname because they were built at

Goswell Hill in 2003. The Windsor gaol
backed on to this lane during the first half of
the nineteenth century. (BM)

slight angles to each other. The shop at the corner of St Leonard's Road and Clarence Road was long referred to as Crosses Corner although seed-merchant G R Cross had ceased to trade there during the 1960s. The public house across the road formerly known as The Hope, now calls itself Crosses Corner. Some of these colourful names have fallen from use, but others have been adopted and thus perpetuated, such as Crosses Corner. Another one is Madeira Walk, a path on the north side of Bachelors Acre, a reminder of the time when people, including visitors to the old Infirmary between Bachelors Acre and Victoria Street, had leisure to sun themselves there and dream of warmer climes.

(PM)

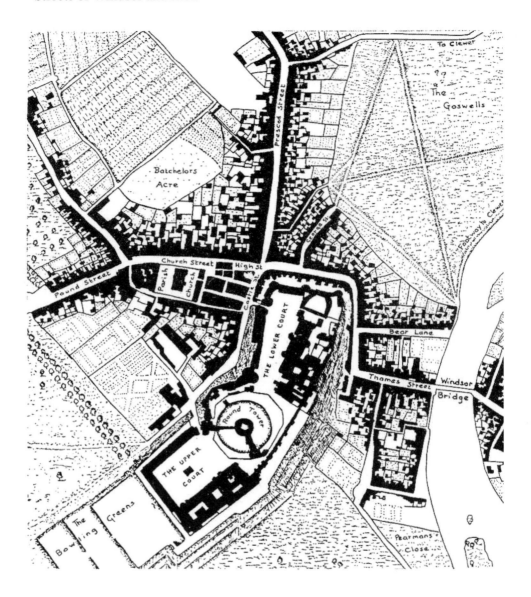

Part of Collier's Map of Windsor 1742 (redrawn)

Note Park Street is called Pound Street, River Street was Bear
Lane and Station Approach was George Street.(JH)

And all the rest

Inevitably a small number of street names do not fit into any of the earlier chapters. Three – East and West Crescent and North Close – simply referred to the location of the roads within the housing estate. Relief Road explains the main function of this modern road. Orchard Avenue was so named because there had once been an orchard in the area before it was developed. Goslar Way commemorates the fact that Windsor is twinned with the German Town of Goslar, and Orwell Close was built on the site of Orwell House, one time home of Lady St Leonard's. Fairlight Avenue is on the site of Fairlight House, and Dower Park on the site of the Dower House of St. Leonard's

Illingworth was named after England's cricket captain of the 1970s, who was much admired by a councillor, and Buckland Crescent commemorates the old established estate agent of that name, since merged with another company.

BUCKLAND & SONS
(ESTABLISHED 1826)
ESTATE AGENTS, AUCTIONEERS
SURVEYORS AND VALUERS
8 High Street, WINDSOR
Tel.: WINDSOR 48 & 1722
Also at
SLOUGH (Tel. 21307/8), Reading
And 4 Bloomsbury Square, London

Buckland's Advertisement 1953

Chaucer Close is a recent addition to the town, but the name is that of the medieval poet Geoffrey Chaucer, famous for his *Canterbury Tales*, but he had an important connection with Windsor. He was appointed Clerk of the Works at St George's Chapel in 1390 when it was found to be unsafe and had to be rebuilt. Another writer commemorated is Lord Byron in Byron Court. Winch Terrace at the western end of the town was named after a family that farmed in Dedworth in the seventeenth and eighteenth centuries, and Sutherland Grange was the home of the Duchess of Sutherland and her new husband Sir Arthur Rollitt MP. The Duke of Sutherland had previously owned The Willows next door. There are still many willow trees in the grounds.

Sutherland Grange in the 1940s (RBMC)

In contrast there is a much larger group which have defied all our attempts at a local explanation. Many of these are on estates built by private developers with no local allegiance who may have drawn their names from a personal list, and the council list includes many distant towns such as Helston Lane (Cornwall). Other street names that could be derived from places are:

Birchington Road (Kent)   Shirley Avenue (Birmingham)
Burnham Close (Bucks)   Stirling Close (Scotland)
Dorset Road   Stroud Close (Gloucestershire)
Duncannon Crescent (Wexford)   Wilton Crescent (Wiltshire)
Haslemere Road (Surrey)

The Willows in the 1940s (RBMC)

It is possible to speculate on the reason for some names. Was Stephenson Drive named after the locomotive engineer of that name or Captain Henry Frederick Stephenson, the arctic explorer who had links with Clewer? Was Wyatt Road named after the architect who remodelled the castle for George IV? It should surely have been possible to link St George's Close with St George's Chapel, but the former presence of a group of houses with the same name not far away in Dedworth Road clouded the issue. The same kind of difficulty made us doubt the possible explanation for the naming of White Horse Road. Was it named after the close of that name in Windsor, shown on the inclosure map? Or could it have been a twist on the name of the public house across the road – the Black Horse? Was Fountain Gardens so named because it is close to the former site of a fountain in Osborne Road? And was there any connection between the Templars Hall, which became the Labour Hall but is now scheduled for redevelopment, and Temple Road?

We offer no explanation for the following:

Almond Close
Bruce Walk   Frances Road
Brudenell   Hemwood Road
Cinnamon Close   Kentons Lane
Coombe Hill Court   Mayfield Drive
Deacon Court   Rutherford Close
Fairlawn Park   Sawyers Close

Sawyers Close at Dedworth (PM)

The streets of Eton town

Eton is included in this survey of street names because it is such a close neighbour of Windsor. But only the town is dealt with; Eton Wick and the outlying lanes of the parish are omitted, as are the one or two streets which have now vanished.

Though Eton dates from Saxon times and was important enough in the Middle Ages to have both a fair and a market, it has remarkably few streets. It is essentially a town rather than a village but is so small and compact because it has not been able to spread, partly for historical and partly for geographical reasons. On the south and east it is bounded by the Thames; over the meadows to the west Lammas rights – an ancient form of common grazing – have survived against all the odds from Saxon times; while to the north the powerful institution of Eton College has, since the fifteenth century, blocked all but its own expansion.

The majority of the roads and streets of modern Eton appear on the earliest surviving map, that published by William Collier in 1742, but many of them are far older than that.

The High Street, the one major thoroughfare, is thus more important even than in most towns. The word 'high' in this connection has nothing to do with altitude but derives from the old term 'highway', usually 'the king's highway' and came into general use for the principal street of a town only in the first half of the nineteenth century. Before that, Eton High Street was simply Eton Street or The Street or The King's Way, mentioned at least as early as 1315.

(SBc)

The numbering runs southward down the east side and then northwards up the west – the system used when numbering first became necessary because letters were to be delivered to houses instead of being collected from the post office, about the middle of the nineteenth century. (Delivery to all houses in the country did not come in until 1887. The system of having odds and evens on opposite sides of the street is a later development.)

Eton High Street from the Bridge over the Thames 2002 (PM)

The Slough Road is a continuation of the High Street, and links Windsor and Eton with the Bath Road (A4) at Slough. It probably follows, at least as far as Willowbrook, the ancient route which must be as old as the first regular crossing of the Thames at Eton, whether by bridge or ferry. It might even be pre-conquest, since Eton was certainly an organised Saxon settlement, with well-used tracks connecting it with other ones. Or it could date from William the Conqueror's founding of Windsor Castle in 1070, as communication with his next castle to the north, Berkhamstead, would have been essential. Certainly it was in use by the late twelfth century if, as is almost certain, there was a Windsor bridge by then. This road was notoriously muddy in the sixteenth century, and probably in all ages up to the laying of a good Victorian surface; Bardolph, in *The Merry Wives of Windsor*, says 'as soon as I came beyond Eton they threw me off in a slough of mire'. The road became a turnpike in 1766 and remained one until 1870.

Eton Wick Road follows the line of one of the footpaths which ran westward from the town to the Wick, where the farms and commons lay. It was known more often as the Dorney road until well into the nineteenth century, when Eton Wick developed considerably. The first large scale Ordnance Survey map in 1868 branded it as Etonwick Road, and Eton Wick Road it has remained. It has only one short street branching off it – Willow Place, which is itself a modern name taken from the Willow Tree public house which from about 1835 until 1975 stood at that point on the road almost opposite the cemetery. The small group of nineteenth century cottages were named on maps of the period simply as part of an area called Cottonhall (now the name of a College boys' house) or Folly Bridge; some on the main road survive but Willow Place itself consists of new buildings in a short spur of road.

A few other names have self-evident origins – Meadow Lane and South Meadow Lane run along two adjacent edges of South Meadow, an important area of permanent pasture, and Mill Lane went to the watermill which had been on or near the same site since Domesday Book and earlier. It was powered by the fall of water in the narrow arm of the Thames running between two islands later known as Cutler's Eyot (or Ait) and Tangier Eyot. The water works were established nearby in 1701 and also have the name Tangier.

Mill Lane was re-named Tangier Lane when it was developed with houses from 1839 onwards, though in common parlance the old name continued in use. The origin of this unusual name is obscure. It was certainly in use in Eton before 1742 when it appears on Collier's map and it is tempting to connect it with the North African port which came to the crown in 1663 in the dowry of Catherine of Braganza, Charles II's queen. But it was only held for about twenty years, and no connection of the name with Eton has been found so far*.

Tangier Mill as shown on an 18th century print (SB)

The somewhat unimaginative names Eton Square and Eton Court indicate a certain period in the development of the town: They are neither the meaningful names, often picturesque to us, which have come down from the Middle Ages or relatively soon after, nor are they the deliberate choice of some relevant historical name which is a frequent habit now – they were simply workaday descriptions of the areas. Eton Square was first developed in the 1840s on land which up till then had been gardens and fields; the last of its original buildings, other than the New Inn, have recently been pulled down. Eton Court is now a street, formed when the Baldwin Institute was built in 1911; before that, a long court of the same name, with ancient cottages on the north and a slaughterhouse at the west end, stretched back to South Meadow.

A varied group of local notables are remembered in Baldwin's Shore, Brocas Street, Keate's (not Keats) Lane and King Stable Street, if it is not impertinent to refer to the monarch as local. The original Baldwin is lost far back in the mists of time, the nearby Baldwin's Bridge having borne his name at least as early as 1274 (though since the seventeenth century it has more often been called Barnes Pool Bridge). The Brocas family held estates in Windsor, Dedworth and Clewer from the early fourteenth century, and land in Eton at least by 1337; Brocas Toft, whose rent in 1472 was a red rose at the Feast of the Nativity of St John (24th June, a good season for roses), must have been part of the large field bordering the river to the west of the town, and which is still called the Brocas. In 1569, when the meadow was held by the college from the monarch, one Philip Wilde was paid twelve pence 'for making the two waies for the quene's majestie to pass through Brockess'.

Keate's Lane was named after the famous and fiery little headmaster of Eton College in the early nineteenth century, but it seems likely that Keate House, built about 1785 and standing at the corner where the lane turns into the Eton Wick Road, was named first, and the lane named after the house. Unfortunately the first Ordnance Survey map to show street names, in 1868, made the error of printing Keats for Keate's, and the mistake has stuck.

Dr Keate

King Stable Street – which used, more grammatically, to be written King's Stable Street – gets its name, not surprisingly, from the royal stables, which for centuries stood on a site between the street and the river. The earliest reference so far found dates from 1511 and the latest from 1754, though the crown still held land here, probably that on which the stables stood, until 1819. It might seem odd that the monarch should keep any of his (or her) horses so far from the castle and on the other side of the river. The most likely explanation lies in the condition of Windsor Bridge, a shaky timber structure that somehow, with endless patching-up, lasted until 1819. From 1236 onwards there are innumerable references to its need for repair and in 1277 it was said to be in such a ruinous state that it was unsafe for either laden horse or cart to cross it. Similar complaints occur down the centuries; so possibly the heavy baggage carts of royal luggage and goods coming from north of the river stopped at the stables in Eton, to be taken over the bridge or by ferry in smaller loads.

Sun Close, part of the much larger sun estate, was the block of land on which the row of houses, now numbered 126-137 High Street, was built in the late 1830s. Previously it had been considered too wet to be developed. The short stretch of road on its southern edge used to be called Sun Lane but is now Sun Close. The Sun public house (where George III is said to have enjoyed a tipple on occasion) must surely be connected though it was on the opposite side of the High Street, now No.12.

Church Close is a creation of the 1960s when the college built two masters' houses looking over South Meadow, and metalled the track running alongside the parish church grounds to reach them.

Atherton Court is now a group of three blocks of flats rather than a street as such, but it takes its name from a short street of small nineteenth century cottages of the same name which was always known as Pump Alley, because the communal washhouse with its pump was there. The Athertons, one of Eton's families of clay-pipe-makers, had their workshop at the end of the alley – the process needed a good deal of water – and their name became the official one for the street.

The origin of the name of Sunbury Road, first recorded on the 1839 tithe map, has not so far been found.

Indeed Tangier was not long in British hands, but it was an important acquisition at the time, and the first overseas territory to be garrisoned. For this a new regiment had to be raised, the 1st of Foot or Royal Scots. Two schoolmasters were sent to Algiers, one a Cambridge graduate, to set up the first ever school for soldiers and their children. (the editor)

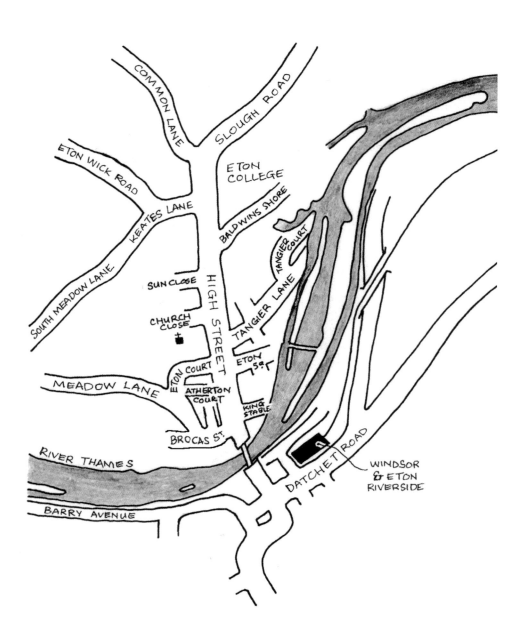

Eton 2003 (CG)

The village of Old Windsor

In 1086, when the Domesday Book was compiled, Old Windsor was the third largest town in Berkshire, and archaeological excavations have shown it had already been inhabited for some three hundred years. It owed its position to the presence, near to the parish church, of a building variously described as a royal hunting lodge and as a palace. It was certainly a place to which the king and the court came periodically, primarily to hunt in Windsor Forest.

When Windsor Castle was completed, the building at Old Windsor became redundant, and there is today no visible trace of the community which once surrounded the parish church. There were two other centres of population, one around the village green, where the Fox and Castle public house and some cottages survive, and the other by the bend in the river now the site of the Bells of Ouseley public house.

In medieval times Old Windsor produced and exported tiles and bricks and from this derives the area of Peter's, previously Pitter's Hill, behind St Peter's School, where clay pits supplied the raw materials.

Old Windsor was always popular as a dwelling place for court servants, such as the Tyle family, and in the eighteenth century became the site of several gentlemen's houses which created employment for villagers.

From the late 1940s onwards building has taken place on every available piece of land and the population now exceeds 6,000. Where possible the parish council have encouraged the use of street names which reflect the history of the village.

Kingsbury Drive takes us farthest back in history for although a  modern road, the name refers to the royal estate of the Saxon and Norman kings. Here William the Conqueror and his sons William Rufus and Henry I held assemblies at which it was recorded that they 'wore their crown'. This probably means that these meetings combined the functions of law-making as our present parliament does, and the administration of the law, now the function of the courts of justice. Excavations carried out in the 1950s under Dr Brian Hope-Taylor proved that the site of Kingsbury lay south-west of the parish church in the grounds of the house called The Priory. The Kingsbury beast (left), a tiny decorative item, was found during the dig. There is a tradition that the ancient track which ran south-westwards from St Luke's Road to the Crown Estate once led from Kingsbury to the royal hunting grounds in Windsor Forest. In later centuries it was known as Miller Lane, and also as Lover's Lane, and Spook Alley in more recent times.

Church Road has probably always been known as Church Road simply because it led to the parish church. The first church at Old Windsor was dedicated to St Andrew, but Edward the Confessor extended the dedication to include St Peter. Both dedications were remembered in street names – St Andrew's Close and St Peter's Close. Land owned by the parish church was known as the glebe and this was commemorated in Glebe Road.

The manor of Tile evidently gave its name to the family of Tile or Tyle. Two of the windows in the parish church are associated with the Tyle family. One which retains some original glass, shows the Tyle crest of two winged dragons with entwined necks. The other displays the initials of Thomas Tyle, who died in 1389. The family still held the manors as late as 1600, and the name was retained in Tyle Place, possibly the site of the manor house. The tile-making industry in this area probably dates back to Roman times, but it was most prosperous during the thirteenth to sixteenth centuries. In 1865 two Roman tombs of the third century AD, known as tile tombs and containing pottery, were discovered at Tyle Place Farm.

'The Village' Old Windsor (DH)

There are in Old Windsor several names of houses which suggest an ecclesiastical connection: The Priory, The Friary and Cell Farm. These derive from the estate of Richard Bateman who lived in The Priory and indulged in the eighteenth century fashion for Gothic fantasy, establishing an order of 'Monks of Runnymede' among his friends, and importing a hermit, a bishop's tomb and various other apparently religious artefacts. The names that remain are the legacy of his creations.

The Inclosure Map of 1817 shows the pattern of roads as they must have existed for centuries, with the addition of the new roads defined by the inclosure commissioners. Most of the roads are named, but many of these names were later changed. The village road, as it was often referred to by local people was shown on the map as Windsor Road, appropriately enough, for until this period it was the main road leading to the town of Windsor from the village, before the Straight Road was laid out. Later in the century, Straight Road was said to be a favourite drive of Queen Victoria. She could call at the Royal Tapestry works, or continue on to Runnymede, her progress noted from the Round Tower by the little white cloud of dust along roads virtually free from traffic. Tapestry Hall reminds us today of the Royal Tapestry works.

Tapestry Hall 2003 (BM)

Today the village road is known as St Luke's Road and Burfield Road. Why the mission church of St Luke's should be dedicated to the Greek physician saint is not clear, but a mission church has stood on the site for over a hundred years. (PM)

Burfield Road took its name from one of the four common fields – Burghfield, Eldersfield, Northfield and Hamfield. These common fields remained intact until the early nineteenth century when they were divided by authority of the Inclosure Acts. Hamfield lay in the northern part of the village in the area known as Ham Island, reached appropriately by Ham Lane. The word 'ham' means a meadow, and much of this land so close to the river must have been water meadow. Meadow Way and Meadow Close were built on the meadow which was once crossed by a public footpath from Straight Road to Church Road. Cell Farm Avenue was built over the land of Cell Farm; the building in Church Road is thought to be in part pre-eighteenth century but is now divided into five houses.

Tudor Lane was built on part of the grounds once belonging to the house that was known as Tudor Lea. Ousley Road is more difficult to explain though many different theories have been suggested. TE Harwood explains its meaning:

'With the numerous *Leys* along this stretch of the river Thames, to distinguish Old Windsor *Ley* from others, people who used the river called it *Ooze-ley* because of its natural characteristics.'

Crimp Hill Road is an example of a street name that has proved impossible to explain. Union Corner at the junction of Crimp Hill Road and Burfield was formerly known as Stocks Corner because the village stocks once stood there. The name was changed to Union Corner when London buses came to the village, enabling people to alight at a convenient point for visiting the Union Workhouse.

The workhouse became King Edward VII hospital, and catered originally for maternity gynaecology and premature babies, as well as the geriatric wards and the part III old people's accommodation in the main building. It has now been converted into houses. The parish council was keen that the name Bear's Rails should be used to commemorate the bear pit inside Windsor Great Park nearby, where in the eighteenth century bears were kept for bear baiting. It was amusing to be told by the young lady in charge of sales at the development that they were happy to use the name Bear's Rails Park if it could be guaranteed that there had been no cruelty to the bears!

Bear's Rails Park 2003 (BM)

Royal connections are to be seen in the names Queens Close, built at the beginning of the reign of Queen Elizabeth II, and Kingsbury Drive which was built at the same time but commemorates the Anglo Saxon building. The Albert Road to Windsor, named after the Prince Consort, was built in 1851 to replace the road through Frogmore, which was thought to intrude upon the royal family's privacy. In 1878 Prince Leopold, Duke of Albany became president of the Old Windsor Tapestry Manufactory, and many of the weavers brought over from France lived in Albany Road.

The trend of the eighteenth century for the gentry to take up residence in the village is also reflected through the street names. Clayhall Farm was inherited by Mrs Laura Keppel (the widow of the Hon Frederick Keppel, Dean of St George's and later Bishop of Exeter) from her father Sir Edward Walpole. In 1785 Sir William Herschel the discoverer of Uranus and court astronomer to George III, moved into Clayhall. He started to work on the great 40ft telescope but it was never to be finished at Old Windsor because he found Mrs Keppel 'litigious, unhelpful and impossible'. She was once described by her uncle Horace Walpole as a 'fiery furnace'. Herschel moved out in less than a year to Slough. From this we find the origins of the names of Clayhall Lane, Keppel Spur and Walpole Road. Nearby Grove Close has no association with Walpole.

The original Pelling House, from which came Pelling Hill, was built by Francis Pigot MP in the second half of the eighteenth century and named after his uncle Canon John Pelling of St George's. Henry Jeffrey Flower, 6th Viscount Ashbrook, a personal friend of George IV, owned Beaumont Estate from 1805 until his death in 1847. He had Ashbrook Road named after him, married twice and had a large family, most of the children being born at

The Grange, Old Windsor (DH)

Beaumont. His widow sold the estate to the Jesuits in 1854; Priest Hill was later named after the Jesuit priests. Follett Close was named after Colonel and Lady Follett who lived at Woodside towards the end of the nineteenth century and the beginning of the twentieth. They did much for the village. Colonel Follett was churchwarden and read the lessons for many years in the parish church. Aylesworth Spur runs off Ashbrook Road, but the significance of this name is not known.

Lyndwood Drive was built on the site of Lyndwood House and grounds. Randall Court was named after Mr Randall, the last owner of Lyndwood House. Mills Spur was named after Mr Mills who lived at Elmlea, later the Malt House, and this is commemorated by Malt House Close. The Mills family lived in Old Windsor for over 400 years. Ricardo Road takes its name from Francis Ricardo who owned the house known as The Friary, now divided into flats, and Orchard Road was built on the site of his orchard.

Newton Lane and Newtonside take their names from a large house Newton Court, which stood in Burfield Road. It had formerly been The Grange, the home of Sir Charles Murray KCB (1806-1895) diplomat and traveller and friend of Edward VII. It was at the Grange that Edward regularly met Alice Keppel, his mistress. It subsequently became a hotel, the headquarters of an insurance company and then a nurses' home. A small road, Cornwell Road, was built on part of the recreation ground and named to commemorate a former publican of the nearby Fox and Castle. Later Newton Court was itself demolished and the road called Newton Court was built there.

Harwood Gardens along with the Ashbrook Road estate stand on the thirty acres of grounds once belonging to Burfield Lodge. In the 1920s the Lodge belonged to Mr Pilkington-Shaw, a deputy lieutenant of the county; his son J A Pilkington-Shaw lived there until the end of the Second World War. Shaw Court, a block of old people's flats, was named after these two men. Harwood Gardens was named after the Rev Thomas Eustace Harwood, who worked at Old Windsor as assistant curate from 1862 to 1873 and as vicar from 1876 to 1911. His son Eustace Harwood wrote the book *Windsor Old and New,* which was published in 1929, to the memory of his father. Warrington Spur recalls another vicar of Old Windsor, the Rev William Warrington. He worked at the parish church from 1789 to 1824; a monument to him was placed on the belfry wall.

William Ellis was the headmaster of the village school from 1901 to 1934, a much-loved man who was organist and choirmaster for many years at the parish church and William Ellis Close is named after him.

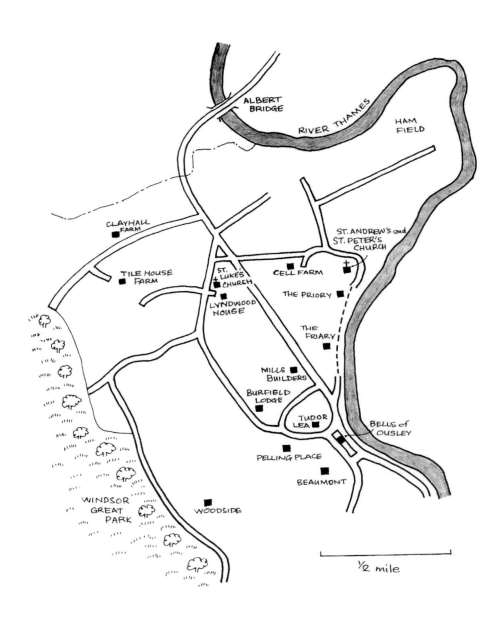

Old Windsor c. 1851 (CG)

Gregory Drive and Pollard Close are two roads where the parish council was unable to influence matters. The builders of the houses named them both. Lime Tree Court was called after the limes which were saved when the houses were built. Farm Drive, Ham Lane and Malt House Close have obvious connections with the buildings or land on which they were built.

Three recent developments commemorate local councillors. Hartley Copse was named after Arthur Hartley who served as parish district and county councillor. Robin Willis Way remembers Dr Robin Willis, parish and county councillor who was killed in a road accident while still a young man, and Gilson Court, a development on the river bank near the Bells of Ouseley, was named after Christopher Gilson, church warden and chairman of the parish council who died in 1986.

(PM)

Windsor streets from the earliest time to the nineteenth century

The earliest known references to these streets, (not necessarily by their present names) are given from 4 main sources of information:

> a) deeds, 13th - 17th centuries
> b) maps, 17th – 20th centuries
> c) directories, 19th – 20th centuries
> d) census returns 1841-1901

In many instances the streets had long been in existence before they are recorded on any surviving document or map. One of the most difficult decisions has been, when is a road a road, and not a track? For the purpose of this index, no definition has been attempted, but where a modern road is shown on the line of an old road or track, this has been recorded in the index, except where it was obviously only a footpath. Every effort has been made to avoid inaccuracies, but in some cases the records themselves are deficient.

Modern Name	Older Name	Deeds	Maps	Directories	Census	Lost
Adelaide Square			1850	1846	1841	
Acre Passage			1742	1858	1841	
Albany Road			1897	1898	1891	
Albert Road			1868	1930	1861	
Albert Street	Alfred Place,		1868	1878	1871	
Alexandra Road	Brewer Street		1742	1861	1861	
Alma Road			1868	1861	1861	
Arthur Road			1897	1875	1871	
Bachelors Acre		1629	1615	1852	1841	
Barrack Lane			1742	1854	1841	1864 (most)
Barry Avenue			1897	1909		
Beaumont Road			1860	1871	1871	
Bexley Street			1868	1868	1861	
Bolton Road	Bone Lane		1761	1846	1841	
Bridgewater Terrace			1868	1890	1881	
Brook Street			1742	1830	1841	
Castle Hill	Park Hill, Castle Street	1662	1607	1811	1841	
Charles Street			1860	1854	1841	
Church Lane	Church Street	1340	1607	1811	1841	
Church Street	Fish Street	1422	1607	1811	1841	
Claremont Road			1839	1854	1861	
Clarence Clump			1860	1898	1861	1960s
Clarence Crescent			1839	1838	1841	
Clarence Road	New Road		1839	1838	1841	
Clewer Court Road	Lime Close	1384	1761	1968		
Clewer Fields	Church Path		1839	1846	1841	

Clewer Hill Road	Clewer Green		1761	1846	1841	
Clewer New Town			1868	1900	1901	
Dagmar Road			1897	1891	1881	
Datchet Road	Datchet Lane, Mill Lane	1552	1607	1811	1841	
Dedworth Road	Dedworth Green, New Road		1761	1846	1841	
Denmark Street	Victoria Cottages		1868	1898	1871	1960s
Devereux Road			1881	1898	1891	
Distill House Row			1868	1898	1841	1926
Dorset Road			1868	1861	1861	
Duke Street	St Andrew's Road, Gardeners Cottages		1897	1891	1871	
Edward Square	Victoria Cottages		1868	1898	1881	1960
Farm Yard			1742		1841	
Frances Road			1868	1875	1881	
Frogmore Road			1607	1830	1841	1850
Garden Court			1868	1898	1841	1926
Garfield Place	Gospell Lane		1868	1898	1891	
Gloucester Place			1868	1846	1861	
Goswell Hill	Goswell Lane		1742	1844	1841	
Goswell Place			1868	1898	1881	1960s
Goswell Road	Gas House Lane		1860	1846	1841	
Green Lane			1897		1871	
Grosvenor Place	Cambridge Place		1868	1871	1891	1960s
Grove Road	Grove Place		1850	1830	1841	
Hatch Lane	Woodhatch Lane		1761	1846	1841	
Helena Road			1742	1890	1871	
Hermitage Lane	Chapel Lane, Clewer Green		1817	1846	1881	
High Street	Market Street, Church Street	13th century	1607	1811	1841	
James Street			1850	1846	1841	
Jubilee Arch	Station Approach, George Street		1742	1830	1841	
Kentons Lane			1812			
Keppel Street			1742	1830	1841	
King Edward VII Ave	Datchet Road / Lane		1850	1859	1841	
Kings Road	Sheet Street		1607	1838	1841	
Love Lane			1742	1846	1841	1916
Maidenhead Road	Surly Hall Road	1607	1839	1846	1851	
Market Street	Butchers Row, The Shambles, Queen Street		1607	1811	1841	
Mellor Walk	Leworth Place		1868	1898	1871	
Mill Lane	Clewer Mill	1384	1817	1830	1841	
Oak Lane	Bexley Terrace		1868	1868	1861	
Osborne Road			1881	1877	1871	
Oxford Road	Clewer Lane / Road	1319	1742	1838	1841	

Street	Former names					
Park Corner			1839	1963		
Park Street	Cuthorse Street, Moor Street, Pound Street	13th century	1607	1811	1841	
Parsonage Lane	Hatch Lane, Rectory Lane		1761	1920	1841	
Peascod Street		13th century	1607	1811	1841	
Peascod Place	Sun Passage		1742	1898	1841	
Prince Consort Cottages	Model Cottages		1868	1854	1861	
Queen Charlotte Street			1742			
Queen's Road			1897	1854		
Red Lion Row			1839	1898	1841	1926
River Street	Bear/Beer/Bier Lane, Bereman Lane	13th century	1607	1823	1841	
Romney Lock Road	Datchet Lane		1742	1811	1841	
Roses Lane	Black Horse Lane		1761	1922		
Russell Street	Chancery Lane	1851	1846	1844	1841	
St Alban's Street	Priest Street	1379	1607	1823	1841	
St Leonard's Ave			1897	1898	1881	
St Leonard's Hill			1761	1830	1841	
St Leonard's Road	Spital Street / Road	1351	1607	1830	1841	
St Mark's Place			1897	1898	1881	
St Mark's Road			1897	1875	1871	
Sheepcote Road	Ash Lane		1817	1947		
Sheet Street		1296	1607	1811	1841	
Sheet Street Road	Shaw Lane		1607	1830	1841	
Sydney Place			1871	1840	1841	1960s
Smiths Lane	Sherbourne Lane	1761	1817	1846	1851	
South Place			1839	1898	1841	1960s
Spinners Walk		1851	1860	1898	1841	
Spring Gardens			1860	1868	1841	1864
Stovell Road			1897	1968		
Sydney Place			1868	1868	1841	1960s
Temple Road			1871	1891	1901	
Thames Side			1607	1830	1841	
Thames Street	Bishop Street, Bridge Street	1312	1607	1811	1841	
Tinkers Lane			1761	1970		
Trinity Place			1868	1854	1861	
Vansittart Road	Vansittart Street		1817	1861	1871	
Victor Road			1900	1898	1901	
Victoria Street	New Road, Victoria Lane		1742	1838	1841	
William Street			1850	1838	1841	
Winkfield Road		1607	1817	1898	1861	
Wolf Lane			1761	1930		

Windsor Streets Since 1900

Abbots Walk	1950s	Charlton	1970s
Addington Close	1960s	Chaucer Close	1990s
Alden View	1960s	Chestnut Drive	1970s
Almond Close	2000s	Cinnamon Close	2000s
Andermans	1960s	Clewer Avenue	1920s
Ash Lane	1960s	Clewer Park	1960s
Aston Mead	1950s	Clifton Rise	1960s
Bailey Close	1970s	College Crescent	1930s
Ballard Green	1970s	Combermere Close	1960s
Balmoral Gardens	1970s	Convent Road	1960s
Basford Way	1970s	Copper Beech Close	1960s
Bell View	1940s	Cranbourne Avenue	1940s
Benning Close	1970s	Cross Oaks	1950s
Birch Grove	1970s	Dawson Close	1960s
Birchington Road	1960s	Dean Close	1960s
Black Horse Close	1960s	Dedworth Drive	1940s
Bolton Avenue	1910s	Dower Park	1970s
Bolton Crescent	1900s	Duncannon Crescent	1970s
Bradshaw Close	1960s	Duncroft	1950s
Bridgeman Drive	1970s	Dyson Close	1940s
Bruce Walk	1970s	East Crescent	1920s
Brudenell	1970s	Edinburgh Gardens	1960s
Bryer Place	1970s	Ellison Close	1960s
Buckland Crescent	1930s	Elm Road	1900s
Bulkeley Avenue	1940s	Errington Drive	2000s
Burnetts Road	1960s	Fairacres	1970s
Burnham Close	1960s	Fairlight Avenue	1930s
Burton Way	1970s	Fawcett Road	1960s
Butlers Close	1960s	Filmer Road	1970s
Byron Court	1990s	Firs Avenue	1960s
Camm Avenue	1970s	Forest Road	1930s
Carey Close	1950s	Foster Avenue	1940s
Carter Close	1950s	Fountain Gardens	1980s
Cavalry Crescent	1970s	Franklyn Crescent	1970s
Cawcott Drive	1970s	Frymley View	1950s
Chantry Close	1960s	Furness	1970s
Chapter Mews	1980s	Fuzzens Walk	1970s

Gordon Road	1920s	Loring Road	1940s
Goslar Way	1960s	Losfield Road	1940s
Guards Road	1970s	Lovejoy Lane	1970s
Gratton Drive	1960s	Luff Close	1970s
Greenacre	1950s	Lyell	1970s
Gwynne Close	1960s	Manor Farm Close	1950s
Hanley Close	1960s	Manor Road	1930s
Hanover Way	1940s	Mansell Close	1940s
Harcourt Road	1960s	Marbeck Close	1960s
Harrington Close	1970s	Martin Close	1960s
Haslemere Road	1930s	Merwin Way	1960s
Hawtrey Road	1960s	Monks Road	1950s
Hayse Hill	1950s	Needham Close	1950s
Helston Lane	1980s	Nelson Road	1930s
Hemwood Road	1970s	Newberry Crescent	1960s
Highfield Road	1960s	Nicholls	1970s
Hilltop	1940s	Nightingale Walk	1990s
Holly Green	1960s	North Close	1950s
Homers Road	1960s	Orchard Avenue	1930s
Hunters Mews	1980s	Orwell Close	1970s
Hylle Close	1960s	Park Close	1970s
Illingworth	1970s	Peel Close	1960s
Imperial Road	1920s	Perrycroft	1950s
Jacob Close	1960s	Pierson Road	1960s
Keeler Close	1970s	Poolmans Road	1950s
Keepers Farm Close	1940s	Princess Avenue	1940s
Kenneally	1970s	Priors Road	1950s
Kimber Close	1970s	Queen Anne's Road	1900s
King Edward Court	1970s	Queen's Road	1900s
Kingsfield	1960s	Rays Avenue	1900s
Knights Close	1960s	Rectory Close	1960s
Lammas Court	1970s	Redford Road	1960s
Leigh Square	1960s	Regent Court	1980s
Liddell Place	2000s	Relief Road	1960s
Little Buntings	1960s	Rowland Close	1970s
Little Woodlands	1980s	Royal Free Court	1990s
Lockets Close	1960s	Ruddlesway	1960s
Lodge Way	1960s	Rutherford Close	1990s
Longbourn	2000s	Rycroft	1950s
Longmead	1960s	Rydings	1950s

St Alban's Close	1970s	Thames Mead	1970s
St Andrew's Avenue	1930s	Tozer Walk	1970s
St Andrew's Crescent	1930s	Tudor Way	1940s
St George's Close	1949s	Tyrell Gardens	1970s
St John's Drive	1970s	Upcroft	1950s
St John's Road	1930s	Vale Road	1920s
Sawyers Close	1960s	Ward Royal	1960s
Selwyn Close	1990s	Washington Drive	1980s
Sherbourne Drive	1950s	Wells Close	1980s
Shirley Avenue	1960s	West Crescent	1920s
Sidney Road	1970s	Westmead	1950s
Sinclair Road	1990s	White Horse Road	1960s
Snowden Close	1970s	Whiteley	1960s
Springfield Road	1950s	Windmill Close	1950s
Stephenson Drive	1970s	Withey Close	1960s
Stirling Close	1960s	Wood Close	1970s
Stroud Close	1970s	Woodland Avenue	1940s
Stuart Close	1950s	Wyatt Road	1960s
Stuart Way	1950s	Sheepcote Road	1930s
Surly Hall Walk	1940s	York Road	1900s
Testwood Road	1960s		

Eton Streets

Pre-Nineteenth Century Roads

Baldwin's Shore
Brocas Street
Common Lane
Eton Wick Road
High Street
Keates Lane
King Stable Street
Meadow Lane
Mill Lane
Slough Road
Tangier Lane

Nineteenth Century Roads

Atherton Court
Eton Square
Sunbury Road

Twentieth Century Roads

Church Close
Sun Close
Eton Court
Willow Place

Old Windsor Streets

Pre-Nineteenth Century Roads

Burfield Road
Church Road
Clayhall Lane
Crimp Hill Road
Ham Lane
Ouseley Road
Priest Hill
St Luke's Road
St Peter's Close

Nineteenth Century Roads

Albany Road
Albert Road
Datchet Road
Straight Road

Twentieth Century Roads

Ashbrook Road
Aylesworth Spur
Bear's Rail
Cell Farm Avenue
Cornwell Road
Follett Close
Glebe Road
Gilson Court
Gregory Drive
Hartley Copse
Harwood Gardens
Keppel Spur
Kingsbury Drive

Lime Tree Court
Lyndwood Drive
Malt House Close
Meadow Close
Meadow Way
Mills Spur
Newton Lane
Orchard Road
Pelling Hill
Pollard Close
Queen's Close
Randall Court
Ricardo Road

Robin Willis Way
Saxon Way
Shaw Court
St Andrew's Close
The Avenue
The Crofters
The Friary
The Grange
Tudor Lane
Tyle Place
Walpole Road
Warrington Spur
William Ellis Close

Sources

Balance, Selina, *A Town called Eton* (1982).

Bond, M.F., *The Story of Windsor* (Local Heritage Books, 1980).

Bond, Shelagh, *The First Hall Book of the Borough of New Windsor 1653-1725* (RBNW, 1968).

Burrows, Montague, *The Family of Brocas* (1886),

Byrne and Churchill, *Eton Book of the River* (1935).

Calendar of Deeds, Royal Borough of New Windsor Records.

Calendars of Eton and Windsor Deeds, Eton College Records.

Census Returns for Windsor 1841-1901, Windsor Library.

Cuthbert, Elizabeth H., *The Sixth Hall Book of New Windsor* (RBWM, 1984).

Farrar, Henry, Windsor Town and Castle (Hurst village publishing, 1990)

Gelling, Margaret, *The Place Names of Berkshire* (1973).

Gilson, Margaret, *Buildings of Old Windsor* (MF Gilson, 1995)
    A Celebration of Old Windsor (OWPC, 1995).

Harwood, T.E., *Windsor Old and New* (Harwood, 1929).

Hibbert, Christopher, *The Court at Windsor* (Allen Lane, 1964).

Holden's Directory of 1811, BRO.

Hunter, Judith, *Victorian Childhood in Windsor* (1990).

Hunter, Judith, and Marson, Pamela, *The Changing Face of Windsor, 1.The Beginnings* (WLPG, 1977)

Hunt's Royal Windsor Directory 1846, Windsor Library.

Kelly's Directories of Windsor 1926-1974, Windsor Library.

Kelly's Post Office Directory of Berkshire, 1847, Berkshire Libraries.

Knight, Charles, senior, *The Windsor Guide* 1793, 1811 &1815, Windsor Library.

Langton, Jane, *The Second Hall Book of the Borough of New Windsor 1726-1783* (RBNW, 1973).

Macnaghten, Angus, *Windsor and Eton in Georgian Times* (Luff and Co., 1976).
    Windsor in Victorian Times (Luff and Co., 1975).

Marshall's Directories of Windsor 1898-1920, Berkshire Libraries.

Musson and Craven Commercial Directory of Buckinghamshire and the town of Windsor, 1853, Aylesbury Library.

Page, William, ed., *The Victoria History of the Counties of England* (1906-1924).

Piggot & Co. Berkshire Directories for 1830 and 1842, Berkshire Libraries.

Piggot's Directory of Berkshire 1844, Berkshire Libraries.

Register of Electors, Royal Borough of Windsor and Maidenhead, Index of Streets, Windsor Library.

South, Raymond, *The Book of Windsor* (Barracuda, 1977)
    The Fifth Hall Book of the Borough of New Windsor1828-1852 (RBNW, 1974)

Tighe, R.R., and Davis J.F., *Annals of Windsor* (Longmans, 1858).

Underhill, F.M., *Windsor as it Was.* (1972).

Windlesora 1-20, Journal of the WLHPG, 1982-2003.

Windsor: A Thousand Years (WLHPG, 2001).

Maps and Plans

Norden's Map of Windsor Forest, Plan of the Town of Windsor and the Little Park and Plan of Moat Park, 1607, BL.
Plan of the Highe Way from Spittle to Windsor, 1615, St Georges Chapel archives.
Collier's Plan of the Town and Castle and the Little Park, Town and College of Eton 1742, BRO.
John Rocque's Topographical Survey of Berkshire, 1761, copy in Slough Library.
Richard Binfield's Survey of Little Park and Parish of New Windsor, 1785. BRO.
Book of Plans, Royal Borough of New Windsor, 18th and 19th centuries, BRO.
Map of the Parish of Clewer, 1812, BRO.
Plan of Proposed New Roads in Windsor, 1820.
Inclosure Maps and Awards of Clewer, 1817; New Windsor, 1819; Old Windsor, 1817, BRO.
Tithe Maps of Clewer, 1839; New Windsor, 1851: Old Windsor 1842, BRO.
Plan of the Parish of New Windsor, 1850, RBMC.
Plan of Windsor, 1858, RBMC.
Bedborough's Map of New Windsor, 1859. (Private Collection)
Plan of the South Western Part of Windsor, 1860, BL.
Ordnance Survey Maps 6 in and 25 in Series, 1868 onwards, BL.
Map of Clewer 1880, Francis Tress Barry, RBMC.

Abbreviations:

BL	British Library
BRO	Berkshire Record Office
RBMC	Royal Borough Museum Collection
RBNW	Royal Borough of New Windsor
RBWM	Royal Borough of Windsor and Maidenhead
WLHPG	Windsor Local History Publications Group
OWPC	Old Windsor Parish Council

Illustrations supplied by

Drawings by:

SB Selina Ballance
DF Daphne Fido
CG Colin Gray
DH Derek Hart
JH Judith Hunter

Photographs by:

BM Brigitte Mitchell
PM Pamela Marson

Illustrations loaned by:

BHc   Collection of Beryl Hedges
BMc   Collection of Brigitte Mitchell
GTc   Collection of Geoffrey Try
PMc   Collection of Pamela Marson
NMR   National Monuments Record
RBMC Royal Borough Museum Collection
SBc   Collection of Selina Ballance
WSEE Windsor Slough & Eton Express
VS   The Victorian Society

Windsor Local History Publications Group

Windlesora

Copies of Windlesora 1-7 are no longer available from the group, but can be consulted at Windsor Library and are sometimes available second hand. The following are still available.

No 8 (£1.50) Samuel Lillycrop, Canon Carter and the 'Clewer Case', Prince Consort Cottages, Some Windsor Memorials, Stained Glass Windows with Windsor Connections.

No 9 (£1.50) Davies of Windsor, Clockmakers, J. Gane and Co of Eton, Old Windsor Cricket, Football and Working Men's Club, Bier Lane

No 10 (£1.75) Windsor's Riverside, Poor Little Orphans (St John's Home), Joseph Ryder, The First UK Airmail Delivery, Windsor Steam Laundry, Royal Volunteer Review.

No 11 (£2) Robert Keayne of Windsor and Massachusetts, Clewer St Stephens's, Fred Fuzzens' Early Life, Windsor Parish Players, A Schoolboy View of the 1947 Floods, Sophie Elizabeth, Marquise d'Harcourt.

No. 12 (£2) Margaret Oliphant, Cinderella in the Waterloo Chamber, St Augustines Home Clewer, The Chocolate Connection (Caleys).

No 13 (£2) Windsor Boys' School, Bachelors' Acre Tank, Princess Christian Hospital, WG Grace and Cumberland Lodge, Clewer Camera Club, Edward Lear at Clewer Green.

No 14 (£2) Lord Gowrie VC, Windsor Model Aero Club, The Ken Shepherd Archive, Dedworth War Memorial (Belford Alexander Wallis Wilson), "Curtain Up" - The Theatre Royal Programme.

No 15 (2.75) **Our Twenty First Birthday Issue** Mary 'Perdita' Robinson, Theatre Royal and the National Trust, William Morris Stained Glass at Dedworth Church, Alice in Wonderland - the Windsor Connection, Topham Foote and Thomas Reeve, Memoires of the Marquis d'Harcourt, Rise and fall of the Windsor Bank, Harry Greenwood VC, Problems at Queen Victoria's Funeral.

No 16 (£2.75) Edward Matthew Ward RA, The Children's Tragedy, Perambulations of the Parish Boundary 1801, White Bus to Winkfield, Old Windsor Carnival, The Apothecary's Token 1666, Pennyroyal Almshouses.

No 17 (£2.75) Market Cross House, Who Tried to Kill Lady Florence Dixie? Esther Sheridan, Windsor Deceived (Windsor's Hospitals under the NHS), The Beautiful Lady Waldegrave, Lady Florence Paget, From Workhouse to Mansion, Living in the Shadow of Eton College, A Suffragette Attack, The Windsor Chair, Oliver Brooks VC, Congregationalism in Windsor - The Beginnings,

No 18 (£2.75) Passages of a Working Life - Charles Knight, The Creators of the Dioramas, St Peter's School Old Windsor, Denman and Goddard, Mrs Horace Dodge and St Leonard's Mansion, Eton Wick - a Village in the Shadow of Eton, The Reverend Arthur Robins, MA, Debunking a Myth - The Copper Horse.

No.19 (£3.00) **Jubilee Edition** How Windsor celebrated earlier Jubilees. Memories of the 1977 Silver Jubilee. Memories of Wartime and VE Day. Keppel Terrace, a vanished part of Windsor. Leading Councillors in the 19th Century. Obitury Raymond South.

No 20 (£3.00) **Fifties Edition** The First Windsor Rediscovered, The Royal Borough's Glory Days, Clewer and Dedworth in the Fifties, Sugar Ray Robinson and the murder of Christine Butcher. Vale House Clinic, George Street, a vanished part of Windsor.

Copies of *Windlesora* and *Windsor: a Thousand Years* can be obtained from the group at 256 Dedworth road, Windsor SL4 4JR. Please enclose 50p for postage and packing for each Windlesora and £2.00 for *Windsor: a Thousand Years*

Windsor Local History Publications Group

INDEX

A

Abbots Walk 53
Acre Passage 29, 82
Addington Close 70
Adelaide Square 58
Adelaide Terrace 58
Albany Road 60
Albany Road, Old Windsor 100
Albert Bridge 77
Albert Road 58, 77, 100
Albert Street 60
Alden View 45, 65
Alexandra Court 56
Alexandra Road
    11, 29, 42, 56, 61, 82
Alfred Mews 81
Allkins Close 69
Alma Cottages 81
Alma Road 11, 56, 74, 79, 80
Andermans 39
Arthur Road 61, 72, 81
Ash Lane 40, 44
Ashbrook Road 100, 101
Aston Mead 65
Atherton Court 93
Athlone Square 63
Aylesworth Spur 101

B

Bachelors Acre
    26, 56, 80, 81, 83
Back Lane 77
Bailey Close 50
Baldwin's Bridge 92
Baldwin's Shore 92
Ballard Green 56
Balmoral Gardens 60

Barnes Pool Bridge 92
Barrack Lane 10, 74, 78
Barry Avenue 69, 81
Basford Way 68
Bear Lane 32
Bear's Rails Park 99
Beaumont Road 43
Bell Farm Estate 42
Bell View 42
Bell View Close 43
Benning Close 66
Bereman Lane 32
Bexley Street 72, 82
Bexley Terrace 44, 82
Bier Lane 32, 54, 79
Birch Grove 44
Birchington Road 86
Bisshopstrate 30
Blackhorse Close 40
Blackhorse Lane 40
Blackpotts 34
Bolton Avenue 71
Bolton Crescent 71
Bolton Road 71, 82
Bone Lane 52, 82
Boots Passage 61
Bourne 37
Bourne Avenue 44
Bowes-Lyon Close 63
Bradshaw Close 65
Braggs Yard 78
Break-Neck Alley 82
Brewer Street 82
Bridgewater Terrace 44
Bridgeman Drive 66
Brocas Street 92
Brook Street 10, 44
Broom Farm Estate 75
Bruce Walk 88

Brudenell 88
Bryer Place 66
Buckland Avenue 85
Bulkeley Avenue 72
Burfield Lodge 101
Burfield Road 98
Burnetts Mead 39
Burnham Close 86
Burton Way 68
Butcher Row 25
Butler's Close 42
Byron Court 85

C

Camm Avenue 71
Camm House 71
Camperdown House 52
Carey Close 68
Carter Close 50
Castle Hill 25, 30, 77
Castle Street 25
Cavalry Crescent 74
Cawcott Drive 66
Cell Farm 97
Cell Farm Avenue 98
Chancery Lane 82
Chantry Close 47
Chapel Lane 53
Chariott's Place 55
Charles House 63
Charles Street 16, 63, 80
Charlton 75
Chaucer Close 85
Chestnut Avenue 44
Christian Square 63
Church Close (Eton) 93
Church Lane 24, 47
Church Path 82
Church Road 50,

Church Road, Old Windsor 96, 98
Church Street 11, 24, 29, 47
Church Terrace 53
Churcher House 69
Cinnamon Close 88
Claremont Road 50, 60
Clarence Clump 80
Clarence Crescent 58, 80
Clarence Road
    11, 16, 50, 58, 80, 82, 83
Clayhall Lane 100
Clewer Avenue 19
Clewer Court Road 18
Clewer Fields 19, 48, 82
Clewer Green Road 16, 41
Clewer Hill Road 16, 41
Clewer Lane 16, 51, 82
Clewer New Town 19
Clewer Park 19, 50
Clewer Street 16
Clifton Rise 65
College Crescent 52
Combermere Close 74
Convent Road 50
Coombe Hill Court 88
Copper Beech Close 44
Cornwell Road 101
Cottonhall 91
Cranbourne Road 44
Cranbourne Wood 18
Creak's Passage 82
Crimp Hill Road 99
Cromwell Road 101
Cross Oak 39
Cross Oak Field 44
Crosses Corner 83
Curfew Yard 82
Cuthorse Well Street 26
Cutler's Eyot 91

D

Dagmar Road 61
Datchet 13
Datchet Lane 10, 15, 34, 40, 77
Datchet Road 15
Dawson Close 56
Deacon Court 53, 88
Dean Close 68
Dedworth 13, 51
Dedworth Drive 16
Dedworth Green 16
Dedworth Road 10, 16, 58, 82
Denmark Street 81
Devereux Road 66, 67
Distill House Row 79
Dodds Hill 77
Dorney road 91
Dorset Road 86
Dower Park 85
Duke Street 11, 82
Duncannon Crescent 86
Duncroft 38, 39
Dyson Close 66, 67

E

East Crescent 85
Edinburgh Gardens 63
Edward Square 81
Edward VII Gateway 61
Ellison Court 56
Ellison House 56
Elm Road 44
Errington Drive 56
Eton Court 92
Eton High Street 89
Eton Square 92
Eton Street 89
Eton Wick Road 18, 91, 92

F

Fairlawn Park 88
Fairlight Avenue 85
Farm Drive 103
Farmyard 34
Fawcett Road 66
Filmer Road 70
Firs Avenue 44
Fish Street 11, 24
Follett Close 101
Folly Bridge 91
Forest Road 44
Fountain Gardens 87
Frances Road 88
Franklyn Crescent 56
Frogmore Road 9, 77, 78
Frymley View 66
Furness 75
Fuzzens Walk 68

G

Gallows Lane 10, 78
Gallys Road 65
Garden Court 79
Gardners Cottages 69
Garfield Place 82
George Street 43, 72, 78
Gilman Crescent 66
Gilson Court 103
Glebe Road 96
Gloucester Terrace 58
Goblin Lane 77
Gordon Road 74
Goslar Way 52, 85
Gospell Lane 82
Goswell Hill 29, 82
Goswell Lane 37, 81, 82
Goswell Place 81
Goswell Road 16, 81

Goswells 11, 37
Gothic Cottages 82
Gratton Drive 69
Gray Court 69
Green Lane 41
Greenacre 46
Gregory Drive 103
Gropencourt Lane 81
Grosvenor Place 81
Grove Close 100
Grove Place 79
Grove Road 42
Guards Road 75
Gun Street Avenue 82
Gwynne Close 65

H

Haileybury Court 51
Ham Island 98
Ham Lane 98, 103
Hanley Close 65
Hanover Close 63
Hanover Way 54, 63
Harcourt Road 72
Hartley Copse 103
Harwood Gardens 101
Hatch Lane 40, 41, 48
Hatton Hill 42
Hawtrey Road 51
Hayse Hill 66
Haslemere Road 86
Helena Road 61
Helston Lane 86
Hemwood Road 88
Hermitage Lane 53
Hibberts Cottages 82
High Field 37
High Standing Wood 44
High Street 10, 25, 29, 32, 47

Highfield 37
Highfield Road 37
Hilltop 46
Holly Crescent 44
Homer's Road 42
Hunsford Lodge 51
Hunter's Mews 56
Hylle Close 65

I

Illingworth 85
Imperial Court 51
Imperial Road 51

J

Jacob Close 65
James Street 63
Jarratt House 69
Jubilee Arch 63, 78

K

Keate's Lane 92
Keeler Close 68
Keeper's Farm Close 43
Kenneally 75
Kentons Lane 88
Keppel Row 82
Keppel Spur 100
Keppel Street 11, 72
Keppel Terrace 79
Kimber Close 69
King Edward Court 29, 81
King Edward VII Avenue 61, 77
King Field 39
King Stable Street 92, 93
King's Market Place 25
Kings Road 64
Kingsbury Drive 95, 100
Kipling Building 52
Kipling Court 52

Knights Close 66, 67
Knights Place 67

L

Lambton House 51
Lammas Court. 42
Lammas Lane 42
Lammon Street 29
Le Worth 26
Leigh Square 66
Leslie Dunne House 69
Leworth Place 29, 81
Liddell 75
Lime Tree Court 103
Little Buntings 46
Little Datchet Lane 34
Little Lane 77
Locketts Meadow 39
Lodge Way 46
Long Mead 42
Longbourn 51
Loring Road 42
Losfield Road 13
Love Lane 78
Lovejoy Lane 42
Lover's Lane, Old Windsor 96
Lover's Walk 51
Luff Close 66, 68
Lyell 75
Lyndwood Drive 101

M

Madeira Walk 83
Maidenhead Road 16, 82
Malt House Close 101, 103
Manor Farm Close 43
Manor Road 42
Mansell Close 42
Marbeck Close 70
Market House 30

Market Place 30
Market Street 10, 25
Martin Close 74
Maryton House 51
Mayfield Drive 88
Meadow Close 98
Meadow Lane 91
Meadow Way 98
Mechanics Court 82
Mellor Walk 81
Merkatstede 25
Merwin Way 66
Mill Lane 10, 21, 40, 77, 80
Mill Lane (Eton) 91
Miller Lane 96
Mills Spur 101
Moat Park 18
Monks Road 53
Monsell Walk 50
Moor Street 77
More Strate 26
Mountbatten Square 63
Myra Cottages 82

N

Needham Close 65
Nelson Road 74
New Road 82
Newberry Crescent 66
Newestrate 32
Newton Court 101
Newton Lane 101
Newtonside 101
Nicholls 75
Nightingale Walk 70
North Close 85

O

Oak Lane 44, 82
Old Windsor 14
Orchard Avenue 85
Orchard Road 10, 101
Orton 13
Orwell Close 85
Osborne Mews 60
Osborne Road 60, 87
Ouseley Road 95, 98
Oxford Road 16, 80, 81, 82

P

Park Corner 46
Park Hill 77
Park Street
     10, 15, 26, 46, 56, 77
Parsonage Lane 47
Peascod Place 81
Peascod Street
     11, 16, 26, 29, 37, 52, 77, 82
Peel Close 74
Pelling Hill 100
Pemberley Lodge 51
Perrycroft 38, 39, 43
Peter's Hill 95
Pierson Road 70
Pitter's Hill 95
Poke Lane 77
Pollard Close 103
Poolmans Road 43
Pound Street 10, 77
Priest Street 25
Prince Consort Cottages 60
Princess Avenue 63
Priors Road 53
Proctor House 69
Providence Place 79
Pump Alley 93

Q

Queen Anne's Court 63
Queen Anne's Ride 63
Queen Anne's Road 63
Queen Charlotte Street 30, 57
Queen Street 25
Queens Close 100
Queens Road 58

R

Racecourse Road 82
Randall Court 101
Ray Mead 37
Rays Avenue 37
Rectory Close 48
Rectory Lane 47
Red Lion Row 79
Redford Road 54, 65
Regent Court 58
Relief Road 80, 85
Ricardo Road 101
River Street 32, 34, 44, 54, 79
River Thames 13, 34
Robin Willis Way 103
Romney Lock Road 15, 77
Roses Lane 40
Rowland Close 66
Royal Free Court 56
Rubbish Gate 26
Ruddlesway 44
Russell Street 82
Rutherford Close 88
Rycroft 38, 43
Rydings 38, 43

S

Sawyers Close 88
Sefstrate 29
Selwyn Close 53

Shaw 16
Shaw Court 101
Shaw Lane 18
Sheepcote Close 39
Sheepcote Road 40
Sheet Street 10, 26, 37, 67
Sheet Street Road 18
Sheet, the 37
Sherbourne Drive 72
Sherbourne Lane 40
Shirley Avenue 86
Shoots Road 77
Sidney 75
Sinclair Road 70
Slough Road 10, 18, 90
Smiths Lane 40, 71
Smock Acre 39
Snowden Close 66, 67
South Meadow Lane 91
South Place 80, 81
Southlea Road 15
Spinners Walk 42, 81
Spital Road 47, 52, 82
Spook Alley 96
Spring Gardens 78
Springfield Road 42
St Albans Street 10, 25
St Andrew's Avenue 11, 50
St Andrew's Close 96
St Andrew's Crescent 11, 50
St Andrew's Road 11, 82
St George's Close 87
St John's Drive 50
St John's Road 50
St Leonard's Avenue 52
St Leonard's Hill 46, 52
St Leonard's Road
    47, 52, 82, 83
St Luke's Road 96, 98

St Mark's Place 51
St Mark's Road 51, 79
St Peter's Close 96
Station Approach 63, 78
Stephenson Drive 87
Stirling Close 86
Stocks Corner 99
Stovell Road 72, 80
Straight Road 97, 98
Stroud Close 86
Stuart Close 63
Stuart Way 54, 63
Sun Close 93
Sun Lane 93
Sun Passage 29, 81, 82
Sunbury Road 93
Surly Hall Road 16, 82
Sutherland Grange 86
Sydney Place 81, 82

T

Tangier Eyot 91
Tangier Lane 91
Tapestry Hall 60, 97
Temple Road 42, 87
Terrent Court 56
Testwood Road 70
Thames Avenue 34
Thames Mead 39
Thames Street
    15, 30, 32, 43, 44, 61
Thameside 34, 44
The Friary 97, 101
The Grange 101
The Hope 83
The King's Way 89
The Priory 97
The Willows 86
Tinkers Lane 51, 65
Tozer Walk 68

Trevelyan 56
Trinity Place 50
Tudor Lane 98
Tudor Way 54, 63
Tulle Lane 29
Tyle Place 96
Tyrell Gardens 66

U

Union Corner 99
Union Workhouse 99
Upcroft 37

V

Vale Road 82
Vansittart Road 11, 72, 81
Victor Road 61
Victoria Bridge 77
Victoria Lane 82
Victoria Street
    11, 58, 61, 74, 82, 83

W

Walpole Road 100
Ward Royal 11, 16, 63, 80, 81
Warrington Spur 101
Washington Drive 65
Wellington Square 78
Wells Close 69
Wessex Court 63
West Crescent 85
West Mead 37, 39

West Row 78
Westmead 37
White Horse Road 87
Whiteley 65
Wickham House 51
William Ellis Close 101
William Street 54
Willow Place 10, 91
Willowbrook 90
Wilton Crescent 86
Winch Terrace 85
Windmill Close 39
Windmill Field 39
Windsor and Eton Relief Road 18
Windsor Road, Old Windsor 97
Winkfield Road 18, 40
Winton House 75
With(e)y Close 39
Wolf Lane 43
Wood Close 44
Woodhatch Lane 41
Woodland Avenue 42
Wright 75
Wyatt Road 87

Y

York Avenue 58
York Place 58
York Road 39, 58

Z

Zigzag cottages 82

(PM)